TruthFeasting

Ja A. Jahannes

TURNER MAYFIELD PUBLISHING COMPANY

1618 Foxhall Rd.
Savannah, GA 31406

Some of these poems have appeared in the first publication of Truthfeasting in 1990, or in other books by Ja a. Jahannes, including Poems from Pakistan, The Poet's Song, Black Generation, Word Song Poets, or in other publications, including The Black Scholar, Essence Magazine, Phati'tude Literary Magazine, Drumvoices Revue, Savannah Literary Journal, African American Review (AAR), inmotionmagazine, The Journal of Pan African Studies (JPAS), the Black Child Development Institute (BCDI) calendars and several other anthologies of poetry.

Cover art by Ulysses Marshall, www.ulyssesmarshall.com from an original painting owned by Ja A. Jahannes

Library of Congress Control Number: 2012945649
ISBN-10:0984030786
ISBN-13:978-0-9840307-8-1

DEDICATION

To my Mother, Frances; my children,
Gloria, Tkeban, Naftal, Ana, and Sara.
And, to my wife, Clara. Thanks.

CONTENTS

BLACK ROOTS   1
CHAMBER SUITE   3
MOTHER'S HAIR   5
HAIKU FOR SONIA SANCHEZ   7
HAITI IS WAITING   8
IN FIELDS OF HONOR   10
LONG TIME COMING   12
GOD LIVES HERE   14
THESE FLOORS   15
SUNDAY DINNER   16
SANDTOWN   19
BIRTH TO VEIL   21
BIRTH   22
CHANGING   23
INVOCATION   24
DOLL MAKING   25
AMERICAN PRIMITIVE   26
I REMEMBER   27
MARTYRS OF THE REVOLUTION   29
MÁRTIRES DE LA REVOLUCIÓN   31
LILIES AND PAPYRUS   33
WE WERE NEIGHBORS, FRIENDS, AND LOVERS   34
THANKFUL IDENTITY   35
TALKIN' SPHINX   36
WAITING   39
DONE GOT GOOD AND GROWN   41
WITH THIS FAITH   42
I WILL BE FINE IN THE MORNING   49
BOMBAY SPIT   50
AN OLD BARN   52
OVERSEER OF A DREAM CALLED FREEDOM   53
THIS IS HOW HE LOVED   55
EYES TURNED   58
NOTE ON AN URBAN PRINCE   60

I HEAR THE SPIRITS CALL MY NAME   61
DON'T YOU THINK I KNOW MY WORTH   64
ONE-EYED PEOPLE   66
SPOILERS   67
WHITE PEOPLE   68
MAN IN POLYESTER SUIT   70
WHITE NEWSPAPER   72
SONG FOR A YOUNG HERO   73
IS HE BLACK   75
I BE BLACKIN'   76
TOTES   77
A ROAD   78
BAD   79
LAST ONE IN SHOULD BRING THE LIGHT   80
PLACE   82
DON DIED TWICE   83
DRUM   84
WOODEN SOULS   85
RAVENS   86
WALK WITHOUT SHOES   87
MAN   88
DEEP OLD MEN   89
FAREWELL   92
EVEN THE INNOCENT ARE JUDGED   93
ALL THAT WE OWN   94
OLD PAINT   95
EPITAPH TO LOVE   96
CHICK   97
I HEAR YOU MARGARET   98
MY BROTHER ANTONIO   101
ON FRIENDSHIP   105
WHO WOULD SELL A CHILD   106
THE POET'S SONG   107
OLD AGE   108
ONLY GOD   109
THE HASHISH POEM   110
INDIGO LORD   111

KEEP A SMILE	112
LAMENT ON LINCOLN STREET'S PASSING	113
ONE TRAIN GOES THROUGH TOWN	115
THE FACULTY MEETING	116
ADOPTION	117
REACHING FOR THE KEYS	118
MY FACE IS ON FIRE	119
CARTEGENA	120
GENIUS, YES	121
CAMPING	122
TIMES	124
SO YOU WANT TO BE A JACKSON	125
YOU CAME TO HEAR ME POET	126
JUST THE WAY	127
ACCIDENT	128
ALL THE THINGS WE ARE	129
EMPTY BOX	130
BRAND NAMES	131
BURN THE BOX	132
I PLAYED GAMES	134
YOU, TWO	135
WHEN LADIES WHISTLE	136
JAZZ	137
MEASURE	138
SLIDE	139
SHE IS THE SOURCE	140
KNOWING	141
GORÉE	142
NECKBONES	143
THE DEATH OF JESSE JACKSON	145
RAP DANCE	147
RED HEAD HARPIST ON A HORSE	149
BACK	150
SURVIVOR'S CREED	151
THE DAYS OF MY FREEDOM HAVE RUN COLD	152
ETHIOPIA	154
BLUES PLAYER	155
ANGELS WITH WHITE FACES	156

ALL BLACKS ARE AFRICANS   157
MARY OF THE SADNESS   158
PICTURE, PICTURE PAINTED   159
POETS ARE PRECIOUS PEOPLE   160
GARDENS OF STONE   161
TIE   162
BEING BLACK IN MY NEIGHBORHOOD   164
LAMENT ON LINCOLN STREET'S PASSING   165
GLAD LADIES   167
THE OLD NEIGHBORHOOD   168
TRUTHFEASTING   169
MOST OF MY LIFE   170
RAISIN' UP   172
PIG LATIN   173
BLACK ON BLACK   174
WE HAVE BEEN AT SCHOOL ALL DAY   176
PROLOGUE   177
FOURTH OF JULY   178
SEE THAT BROTHER THERE   179
SOLEDAD LADY   181
I CAN'T HEAR NOBODY SINGING   182
BLACK COLLEGE KILLING FIELD   183
TECHNOGLYPS   184
MORNING'S COMING SOON   185
PLACE OF THE OTHER'S SEE   186
FASHION A NEW WORLD   187
MANDY LO'   188
IN PASSING   189
THE HEMORRHOIDAL SMILE   190
BURY ME NOT   191
HARMONY   192
SOMETIMES LIES   193
EMANCIPATION OCCASION   194
POETS (OR WE REAL BAD)   195
WHO IS HELD HOSTAGE AMERICA?   196
SISTERS GOT TO LISTEN   198
A THANK YOU NOTE TO M. L. KING, JR.   199

NEW YORK CITY 200
THE LAND DOES NOT KNOW WHO OWNS IT 201
PASSING BEYOND VANITY 202
GROWING OLD 203
FOR MY SISTERS WHO WANT TO BE FREE 204
ROOTED 205
JESUS OF THE FAVELA 206
THE GHOSTS OF WAR 207
YOUR SMILE, YOUR STYLE 208
IF WE FORGET 209
WHEN I FELL 211
BLACK GENERATION 212
IF THEY CUT DOWN THE TREE 222
LITTLE DARK-EYED GIRL 223
KEEP THE DREAM 224
LOOK BACK IN SHAME 225
DREAM MAKER 226
AIN'T I SOMETHING 227
KING CAT AND ALL THAT 228
GOD 231
MY CHILDREN HAVE NEVER KNOWN PEACE 232
ON THE JOY OF READING TO YOUNG BLACK
CHILDREN 234
TOGETHER 235
AUTHOR 236

BLACK ROOTS

They say
I died.
Dark vines
Climb through my sidewalks,
Musty old wood rots in my walls.
They say
That poverty,
Illiteracy,
Drugs,
Wasted humanity fill my corners.
They never lived here.
That's why they say what they say.
I live
Even in the new townhouses
That spring up like fire flies
In the night,
Lighting their light
In my history.
I live here and there.
I live
In the stories
They never hear.

I live in black roots
That rise up from this very ground,
Entwining the generations
Of babies, children, parents, grandparents
And great-grands,
Uncles and aunties and cousins
by the dozens,
Stretching forth to new places,
Still searching
For all they left behind.
I live in the mind.

I answer,
I live with dignity and sassy grace.
I live
In the spirit of this place.

I live among the ghosts,
The music on the wind
Turning corners
And witnessing
The still gone
Parties in the streets;
The night enfolding young boys and girls
Talking their jive
Under the lampposts;
The mothers in their aprons hanging
Out clothes on the back lines
To catch the afternoon freshness;
The old men in the crap shoot in the alley;
The preacher making his way to console
The young wife
Whose husband gave his all in a foreign war
Where life was cheap.
Now the wind blows on tomorrow
Which will make its own notes
On these times.
For sure,
I live.

CHAMBER SUITE_____

The first time I saw the sea I was dead,
Too many rum drinks at the island airport bar
And again at dinner with newlywed friends.
She and he loved me differently
But I was too youthfully aroused
To sit reminiscing
With my nature's urges leaping
synaptic barriers.
I drove their car like a jumbee spirit
To the club by the ocean
Where they said things happened.
I smelled the alchemy
of the sea along the coast.
I felt the sea's warm whistling
Sweet/sour/melon/waterweed breath
In my nostrils.
I danced up a glistening sweat
At the thronged club,
Hypnotically, tribally
From nowhere in my conscious memory,
In the waves of moving handsome women
And poetic boys;
Long enough to find you without a map,
Long enough to be at the seaside
pulling off my clothes,
Wading in the water to get soaking wet
As an excuse for unbridled ecstasy.
The waves laughed all the time
as I undressed
In panting serenading rhythms of the night,
Shamelessly
In the undulating chamber suite of the nocturnal tide.
The purifying breezes
Disguised our sensual scents

as we lay on the beach.
The sea was my ally
in this youthful innocent insanity.
The ancient mother
Knows how to keep a young man's secret.
The sea and I sobered up
Together in the rawness of daylight.
The first time I saw the sea I came alive.

MOTHER'S HAIR

I am rooted in Dinquinesh,
Mother
Source
My coarse, strong dark crown
covered my head
Like twisted threads of creation
Boldly I went up the Nile
Turning dark red brown
Witnessing the rising floods of life
Enthroning foundations of civilization
I created adornments that rested
Upon the heads of pharaohs
And wove my way
Into the heads of queens
Then, I took alternate paths
To the icy lands of the north
Where long and thin
I covered over white skin
I turned blonde gold
And an army of browns
To the east I made silky or straight
Long vines of beauty
Before I left the continent
For islands still springing into being
I detoured through my Afrika
Going as south as south is
Making peppercorns and tight ringlets
On the heads of the clever children of God
Who make the barren desert serve feasts
Out now from the islands
I covered the whole of the world
Tangling and entangling
Transformed and transforming
Coloring and contrasting,

Extending, combing, alchemizing
Knowing or unknowing,
When the children of the Earth
Touch their heads
They touch me
Still, I remember myself, wonderful
I am the same as I was
In the valley
In which I was born

"Dinquinesh," in the Ethiopian language of Amharic, roughly
means "thou art wonderful." It is the name given by the Ethiopians
to the fossil hominoid, Lucy, discovered by American
paleoanthropologist Donald Johanson in Hadar, Ethiopia in 1974.
Dinquinesh is a member of an ancient hominoid species–
Australopithecus afarensis–that lived approximately 3.1 million
years ago. The Dinquinesh fossil is believed to be the oldest
hominoid fossil ever found, therefore the prototype of the mother of
human creation. Her hair was described as very thick, dark and
wooly.

*HAIKU FOR SONIA SANCHEZ*____

Wordseer soaring high
Spitting dark fire thunder truths
Exploding love fields

*HAITI IS WAITING*_____
(HAITI AP TAN)

A dark gray mountain of swirling death
Rose to the outer Heavens
Carrying the voices that heard the rumbling
Long before the ground shifted its place
In the Earth
In this unexpected time
nothing returned the same
Nothing claimed the vacant eyes
That looked without knowing
Nothing gave this time and place a name
All were kin to this wilderness of tragedy
The sky did not close over the land
Fresh uncovered dirt spoke to death nearby
Still, there is victory for prophets
Who speak with vision
Nothing can stop the sun from shining
Through hearts that sing
The world turned on a new course
The just and the unjust had no tribunal there
History was written
On the scarred bodies and minds of the poor
We must now build love on love's foundation
We must teach ourselves
To humble ourselves before God
We must erect the future
for the celestial ones
We must erect a tower of action
That needs no language
We must hold yesterday with yesterday,
Embrace tomorrow today
We build Haiti a new shining lasting presence
We must overcome the blinded barren spirits
We must write the future over desolation

And despair
We must build a monument
For which there is no blueprint
Haiti is waiting
I say, Haiti is waiting
I say, Haiti ap tan
Haiti is waiting

IN FIELDS OF HONOR_____
Ballad of Black Soldiers

We fought and died
With courage and pride.
We could not stand to see
The slightest threat
To this land of liberty.
We shed our blood
On every bloody battlefield,
In every bloody war.
We shed our blood
Both near and far
For democracy and sovereignty.
We were the first in France
In the long, mean years of war,
And proudly our decorations
For bravery we wore
Back to the American shore.
At Chateau-Thierry
And Belleau Wood,
We stood.
We were the first to reach the Rhine.
In Asia, Africa and the Middle East,
Across dividing lines,
It was the same each time.
Though not always treated fairly
We rose above our complaint,
Serving Heaven and country.
Seeing what America could be
We clothed ourselves
In the stars and stripes
And fought and died.
No braver men than we
Raised any country's flag.
And that flag still waves

Over the land of the free,
And the home of the brave.
Now lay us low in fields of honor
Where death is bitter sweet.
Forget not the trampling feet,
Brown bodies and crimson blood
That swelled like a tide.
We who fought and died
With pride.
For if we had to do it
Yet again, America,
In the heat of the day
Or the cold of the night,
We would stand and fight.

LONG TIME COMING _____

For Larry Neal

I am still minding, melding
the space between
A reality of lessness in the land of more,
Holding back, blocking black, genius,
creative forces, life,
And the imperfect way forward to wholeness.
Soulness.
I see skies that open through dark alleys
Where formulas are not foolproof for survival.
Long time coming doesn't worry me.
We must press on,
though resisted by mountains,
Towering mounds of ignorance
of human infancy.
Long time coming doesn't worry me.
We must close the consuming places
Between us/spread among us/
deep within us,
And the treasure squandered
in a haunting house-
Of America, slipping/sleeping away today.
We must cultivate the promised terrain
Till the nation is gone sane.
I press on with my love affair with prophecy,
Born in me,
Born in my quest to free consciousness,
And my calling. I claim my black roots
In the soil of this land.
Philly-ed up, Lincoln forged, world framing,
Solemn thinking/loud proclaiming.
I'm not gone.
Be right back.
Be right back.
Cause I got words that work mojo,

Templates that drop on, and drop on.
Long time coming doesn't worry me.
I'm about birth/rebirth/cool clarity.
Long time coming doesn't worry me.
My work is holding,
Yet unfolding.

Larry Neal was a founder of the Black Arts Movement and my classmate at Lincoln University. "Long Time Coming Doesn't Worry Me" is a tribute poem in my memoir/anthology, WordSong Poets.

*GOD LIVES HERE*_____

Roland Freeman's "West Baltimore Remembered" Project

God lives here
Answering our smallest prayer
And he is mighty able
He opens these doors each morning
And puts food on the table
With kindness He lights our day
He keeps the evil one at bay
And throughout the darkness hour
He holds us in his power

*THESE FLOORS*_____
Roland Freeman's "West Baltimore Remembered" Project

I have swept these floors a thousand times
And waxed them on my knees
For I am blessed to be at home
Where I do as I please

SUNDAY DINNER

Roland Freeman's "West Baltimore Remembered" Project

Cornbread was having a conversation
With collard greens and sweet potato pie
At Sunday dinner
Something about cracklin'
And sitting in a seasoned black skillet
Till she was beautifully brown
When collards interrupted to say
How ham hocks made her feel complete
She just liked his flavor
Baked chicken chimed in
That she couldn't make up her mind if she
wanted
Plain dressing or dressy dressing with oysters
And potato salad confessed
A fondness for celery
and a light touch of paprika
Though she did not know
if mustard added much
Marconi, with her three different
kinds of cheese
Sat quietly like a queen for the tasting
And sweet potato pie, lightly spicy
In her cinnamon and nutmeg
Thought all would be well
If ham would move over
so lemonade could find a place
At the table

SANDTOWN

Roland Freeman's "West Baltimore Remembered" Project

I am lonely now
For these places that are gone
I see them here where once they stood home
Holding my youth
And the crossroads of my future
Where streets spoke
Curtained windows peeked out on the world
The whole world
And doors beckoned me
To find family and friends gathered
To chat up long vivid tales
About our living
I am not alone in my loneliness
There are others
Names and remembrances
A tilt of the head
An exaggerated smile
A halting laugh
Sashaying hips
A do-wop corner sound
In the late of the evening
And shared sadness in times of loss
And pain
Like a cup of sugar borrowed
Never to be returned but shared
Nonetheless
As one shares kisses and hugs
And hopscotch and jacks
Sharing memories too
Of grandma's quick eyes
That saw everything at once
As you entered her domain
Where she ruled like a sky of brilliant sayings

17

Meted out just for you
Or so you thought until you heard her speak
Wisdom more profound to her bed
On her knees at night
Asking God to wait on everybody
Like she had him to herself
And our mothers barking orders like captains
To kids who knew better in the first place
Than to try to get away without doing their
chores
Washing their faces
Speaking politely to their elders
Washing the marble steps
So that strangers would find them shrines
To our ethics
To always do more
Better
And faster
And with more rhythmic joy
Than anybody else
In any other neighborhood
And these steps are outposts against
exclusion
For all are welcome to sit up these places
With equal welcome
Only punctuated by the smells
from our kitchens
That calls out to our bellies
To enter the joy of soul satisfied eating
That made our eyes roll up in our heads with
pleasure
I am lonely now
For the penny candy
And wa-ter-me-lon
Sung by the man whose wagon
Made us think we were moving slow
In the city that moved too fast

To find the simple fun
Of jumping rope and shooting marbles
I am lonely now for Sandtown
I am lonely for the me
That moved away while walls came down
And the people wandered
Disappearing to other neighborhoods
That could never have the ties that brought
us back
Each holiday
Each looking for the others' faces
And the sounds
And smiles
And swagger and strut
Of folk that knew something about living
together
About faith
About fellowship
About friendship
And working men
Who would never get rich
But, were proud enough to hold up their
heads
And ask nobody for anything
they did not deserve
I am lonely now for the shows that
everybody talked about
Before the stars showed up at theater
And the crowd was all dressed out like church
'cept they smelled like evening flowers
In their aftershaves and perfumes
I conjure up the long faces of the children
In the back church pews
Waiting to strip off these Sunday clothes
And run up and down the streets
Playing games like hide and seek
Never knowing

The old corners will disappear
as they turn gray
And the small stores and shops will give rise
To new monuments of new times
Where nothing will be familiar
I am lonely for you today, Sandtown
Down in my bones
But I have my memories
My stories and my witness
To keep you living right here, right now

*BIRTH TO VEIL*_____

Giving birth
To life that will carry the line
In the open field of life
Where nothing exceeds this miracle.
This fathered child
Will feed from mother's breast
Never knowing undue hurt
Before the time of rising.
The mother handed down doll-making
Binding mother and daughter
And gentle hand
Cradling sons
To the stitches
And seams,
The invented faces
That reminds us all of time together.
Time remembered,
Changing the ways,
Finding new worship
In selves.
Still the spirits remain the same,
Ours.
Invocation of the elements
Are commanded by the spirit
Fire, Water, Wind, Light
To these are we entrusted
To move life forward
Through the Veil.
And nothing
Should sever this
History from Birth to veil.

BIRTH

From Clara Agüero Ortiz's book project

Alone, giving birth
To life that will carry the line
In the open field of life
Where nothing exceeds this miracle.
This fatherless child
Will feed from my breast
That will never know the father again, dead
Before this time of newness.

CHANGING

From Clara Agüero Ortiz's book project

Changing the ways
Finding new worship
Still the spirits remain the same
Ours

INVOCATION

From Clara Agüero Ortiz's book project

Invocation
The elements
Are commanded by the spirit
Fire, Water, Wind, Light
To these are we entrusted
To move life forward
Through the Veil

DOLL MAKING

From Clara Agüero Ortiz's book project

Handed down doll-making
Binds mother and daughter
To the stitches
And seams,
The invented faces
That reminds us of time together.
Time remembered

AMERICAN PRIMITIVE_____

Dedicated to Cultural Diversity in America

Its
hard
to make
a dead man
see/feel/know.
I'm
gonna
work
my black mojo
anyway,
Against white currents,
Hoping
To help
the dead
breathe.
It's
the only chance
for life.

I REMEMBER

For Sadie Curtis on her 86th birthday

I remember everything I want to remember.
The sound of my feet moving me to and fro
Taking me wherever I want to go.
I remember the sunlight
kissing me on the face,
Sweetly in the midday morn.
I remember times of joy and laughter
in this place,
And the necessary nuisances
of sorrow dawning,
Tucked into my days and years.
I remember sweetly
the fragrance of a long, good life.
Caring, my constant companion,
Though thorns have been in the roses,
and strife.
Each day I hold up Holy hands,
For the Lord has blessed the table before me.
Yes, the guava duff,
Coconut tart, peas soup and doe boy
All give off their delicious scents.
The eyes behold a feast,
But, it's the guests, seen and unseen,
My "Deary," the children and grandchildren,
None for love the least.
School children grown now, name by name,
But my children just the same;
The others smiling or laughing joyously
That delights my dimming sight.
I'd not trade gold or pearls for living.
I read and find stories that come out right,
Not so much taking as giving.
Every night I put on my favorite perfume
Knowing my blessings without number

Nestling in aromatic bliss, quietly I slumber.

MARTYRS OF THE REVOLUTION

Of the Revolution of the People
Colombia, South America

The spirits of the cities of your births
Welcomed your return,
Heroes against oppression,
Expressing our discontent.
They made a horrific ridiculing spectacle,
Hanging you to strike fear
Where fear could not find comfort.
In the witnessing plaza,
before the damning hour,
The first day of February, 1782,
They decapitated you shamelessly,
Losing their heads,
In arrogant public display.
The winds swept the streets that day
Claiming your souls.
Evil in cabal conspired to destroy you,
Not knowing that time
Is the arrangement for everything.
They call now your names in history.
Scattered bones, skulls, hands and feet,
Are not the keepers of the soul.
Where are the names of your defilers?
Vilified footnotes to infamy.
No one remembers
their names, their stations.
Juan Manuel José Ortiz Manosalvas,
You came again to Socorro.
Jose Antonio Galán keeps watch
over Guaduas.
Isidro Molina keeps vigil in Santafé.
Lorenzo Alcantús is in San Gil, still.
The salt they spread on your worldly goods,
Sustains your descendants

who number legions.
The tyranny that ruled
has long since lost its rule.
They say among the families
Today the young ones
Hear the whisper of those winds.
A new Colombia is beginning.

Historical notes by Clara Agüero Ortiz.
Most often revolutions have been started by intellectuals and individuals of the middle class. In 1782, a revolt in the Spanish colony of Nueva Granada, which later became the nation of Colombia, was begun by ordinary poor citizens in reaction to deplorable economic conditions and other oppressive circumstances. On February 1, 1782, the Spanish representatives retaliated by hanging and dismembering the four leaders of the revolt and sending their body parts to their home towns as a warning to others. That affair has been captured in several monuments and plazas around the country and in recent years in a monumental sculpture by Vallejo in the Chicamocha Canyon in Santander, Colombia. The uprising and its heroes are taught with emphasis in the history books of Colombia. "Martyrs of the Revolution of the People" is dedicated to the gallant men who lead the uprising and their memory.

MÁRTIRES DE LA REVOLUCIÓN DE LOS COMUNEROS

Colombia, América del Sur

El espíritu de vuestra ciudad natal
Os dió la bienvenida,
Héroes contra la opresión,
Expresando vuestro descontento.
Aquellos hicieron un espectáculo
ridículo y horrendo
Colgándoos para infundir miedo
Donde el miedo no pudo encontrar consuelo.
En la Plaza Mayor, antes de la hora maldita
El primer día de febrero de 1782,
Os decapitaron sin vergüenza,
Perdiendo vuestras cabezas,
En arrogante exhibición pública.
El viento barrió las calles ese día
Reivindicando vuestras almas.
La maldad conspiró en cábala para destruiros,
Sin saber que el tiempo lo dispone todo.
Vuestros nombres ahora son llamados
en la historia.
Huesos dispersos, cráneos, manos y pies,
No son los guardianes del alma.
¿Dónde están los nombres
de vuestros corruptores?
Vilipendiando notas de pie a la infamia.
Nadie se acuerda de sus nombres, de sus títulos.
Juan Manuel José Ortiz Manosalvas,
regresaste al
Socorro.
José Antonio Galán vigilas a Guaduas.
Isidro Molina mantienes vigilia en Bogotá.
Lorenzo Alcantús, todavía estás en San Gil

La sal que extendieron sobre vuestros bienes
Mundanos,
Mantiene a vuestros numerosos
descendientes.
El terror que gobernó, hace tiempo perdió su Imperio.
Las familias dicen
Que los jóvenes de hoy,
Escuchan el susurro de esos vientos.
Una nueva Colombia ha comenzado.

Spanish translation and notas históricas by Clara Agüero Ortiz, direct descendant of Juan Manuel José Ortiz Manosalvas who was born in El Socorro, Santander, Colombia.

Notas históricas. En la mayoría de las veces las revoluciones son iniciadas por intelectuales y personas de la clase media. En 1782, una revuelta en la colonia española de Nueva Granada, que más tarde se convirtió en la nación de Colombia, fue iniciada por los ciudadanos comunes pobres en reacción a las deplorables condiciones económicas y otras circunstancias opresivas. El 1 de febrero de 1782, los representantes españoles ahorcaron y descuartizaron los cuatro líderes de la revuelta enviando las partes del cuerpo a sus lugares de origen como una advertencia a los demás. Ese evento ha sido capturado en varios monumentos y plazas en todo el país y en los últimos años en la escultura monumental de Vallejo en El Cañón del Chicamocha, Santander, Colombia. El levantamiento comunero y sus héroes se reseñan con énfasis en los libros de historia de Colombia. El poema "Mártires de la Revolución los Comuneros" está dedicado a la memoria de esos hombres valientes que lideraron la revuelta.

THE LILIES AND THE PAPYRUS__
FOR THE ARAB SPRING, MAY 15, 2011

In search of Egypt
In wondrous monuments of antiquity,
And the gold and silver treasures
of the dynasties,
I am brought to tears
To see the lilies and the papyrus
Along the Nile,
In splendid majesty,
Older still,
Growing free.

WE WERE NEIGHBORS, FRIENDS, LOVERS

Dedicated to those who lived in Turner Station, Baltimore County, MD, and especially the Class of 1960 of Sollers Point High School.

We were neighbors, friends, and lovers
Shot marbles, skipped rope,
Played dodge ball and jacks
Made touch football rough and rugged.
Played on the same playgrounds
At the same schools,
Turner, Fleming, Bragg, Sollers Point, and did
Some kissing in the same places
when it got dark.
Baseball games were storms of excitement;
Basketball had its all-stars, too,
with three pointers
Even before the term was invented.
There was hopscotch, pickup sticks,
Hide-and-seek, cowboys and Indians
And crabbing on a sunny day;
The Teen Center and dark,
dark blue colored light
House parties.
Some of us lived Up Turner,
a place with homes
That had their own faces.
Some of us lived in Sollers Homes, where the
Children were tough and determined.
Some of us lived in Ernest Lyons
with row houses
Neatly lined along winding streets
and avenues;
And Sparrows Point, Edgemere
and Back River,

Jewels of communities.
And some of us lived in Day Village
With its courts and its lazy manicured lawns.
And not everybody minded their own
business,
but some did;
Taking the Number 26 trolley
Or the Number 10 bus
We shopped on Eastern Avenue,
then downtown
Baltimore in the high class stores.
In Turner Station we made fashion look good
Every day, plain and fancy.
We had our own hangouts, pool room,
and our
Own "put it on the books" stores.
The numbers, straight
or combinated,
got some of us
a little money and kept a lot of us poor,
And nobody missed the show
At The Anthony Theater on Saturday,
Where they played "Blue Velvet"
like it was the National anthem.
Some of our neighbors
had knock-down-drag-out fights;
The busybodies went to their windows
And peeped and listened.
We made rings of firefly tails and searched
For four leaf clovers
on the sometimes patchy lawns.
None of our teachers were stupid,
But a lot of them were characters.
What made us different?
We never knew
we were supposedly poor, Black
And "disadvantaged."

We thought we were magnificently endowed,
and culturally rich.
Other folks were missing out on not being us.
Our white steps, potted plants,
crisp white curtains
Or long flowing window drapes
Symbolized our royal households;
There were names
we made for ourselves better
Known than our birth names.
Everybody had a place
to go down-the-country
Where their daddies
and mommas came from.
We were thieves of the first order.
We stole out of school
to the Doghouse submarine
shop in broad daylight.
We stole each other's girlfriend
or boyfriend
in basement parties.
We'd steal away to Jesus
on Sunday morning.
We stole our sanity
Right out from under Jim Crow.
We stole all the stuff the school books
Had to teach us
Mixed it with commonsense
and uncommon joy;
We were something simply because we spoke
Ourselves into being.
Neither history nor time can change our story
As neighbors, friends, and lovers.

*THANKFUL IDENTITY*_____

Kwansabas for Haki K. Madhutbuti
from the 50th Anniversary of Margaret Walker
Alexander's *For My People*

The brother stood. He speaks most clearly;
Across Sonia, Ossie, Mari, joyce, and, Jerry.
Being who we know him to be.
We soar with poetry's tall, gifted Haki.
Gallant griot guide of light and power,
Winging words, eyeing fists, arming voices. Seeking.
Black thunder in truth's high tower. Speaking.

*TALKIN' SPHINX*_____

Kwansabas for Eugene B. Redmond

master drum voice in sacred soular spaces,
talkin' out. callin' our strong black dance,
soaring spirit walker. hymn singing, life chance.
song maker, day breaker from dark nights,
signing us talkin' rights in clear lights.
mojo lifting high paths we never heard.
our talkin' sphinx, riddlin' the wise word.

*WAITING*_____

I've been waiting too long to say
what must be said
I've been waiting to find the words
I've been waiting to tell you
something about me so you
can know something about you
I've been waiting too long to say I love you
Yes, white man I love you
I been waiting
to say that because it frees me
It frees me of hating you
I've been waiting
to free you from the childish things
you have done to me
I've been waiting
to free you from the insanity that
propels you to that dark deserted closet
High up on the hilltop of truth
where you cannot come
down without finding light
I've been waiting
too long to let my poetry begin to
orchestrate your redemption
I don't need the brass of the symphony;
I don't need the strings
I need the cymbal
to sound the end of my waiting
Wake up, this is not a dream you can televise
Wake up, this is not a redundant news feed
It is the reality of the end of waiting
Wake up this is not on Fox, CNN, or BET
Wake up; this is not on your IPod or Kindle
Now it's your turn
I will not wait for you
I will turn in my eyes of hatred

I will stop
Stop
Stop
Waiting right now

*DONE GOT GOOD AND GROWN_*

For poet Malkia M'Buzi Moore

Hey girl,
You know you grown, girl,
See you throw that head
Sway those hips
Move like you own a piece of the rock,
Speaking torrents of truth with your eyes,
Making them weak with your woman power.
Traffic patterns stop when you venture out.
You know it, girl,
You know what you have done
for your man/men,
Your child/children,
Your friends/tribe.
You have liberated prisons
with your presence,
And locked out evil jealousies,
And if we could just see inside your mind,
We'd see you living large
on your half century,
'Cause you know where you been,
Know where you are,
Got a damn good idea where you need to be,
And we know you got nerve enough
To throw your own party.
Girl, you got GOOOOOOOOOOD
And Grown.

*WITH THIS FAITH*_____

"With This Faith" is an excerpt from the oratorio, **With This King – Requiem For Martin Luther King Jr.** performed originally in Savannah, GA in January, 2008, with libretto by Ja A. Jahannes. The work has traditional gospel interludes between narrated sections and instrumental accompaniment.

From all the prophets of yesterday
Came the call,
From Amos,
From the Apostle Paul,
From Jesus the Christ,
Through Mahatma Gandhi, the ascetic,
Came the call
To him, to him.
In 1955, testing the waters -
When Rosa Parks refused to sit
at the back of a bus-
To him
Came the call
To lead the Montgomery Bus Boycott.
To him,
A twenty-six year old preacher,
Came the call,
Not to listen to the voice, but to be the voice
Of prophecy;
Not to listen to the voice, but to be the voice
Of transformation;
Not to listen to the voice, but to be the voice
Of spiritual courage.
In this age
To the present generation of men,
In this age
To speak the Word
That men's hearts would be pricked.
In this age

To speak the Word
That the consciences of the wicked
would be pierced.
In this age
To speak the Word
That principalities of hate and greed
Would throw off their quilts of discord
And heed the call.
Son of a preacher man,
Son of Reverend Martin Luther King, Sr.,
Who was the son of a preacher man.
The Word was in him.
Son of Atlanta, Georgia.
Son of Selma, Alabama.
Shepherd of Dexter Avenue Baptist Church.
Called at twenty-four to pastor.
Son of Ebenezer Baptist Church,
His father's pulpit.
His text was taken from Benjamin E. Mayes -
Educator, social activist, Phi Beta Kappa.
He was a Morehouse College man.
His classroom was the meeting halls
of the South,
And Chester Crozier Theological Seminary.
He drank from the fountains
of Systematic Theology
At Boston University,
Receiving the doctorate of philosophy;
Moved by his teachers,
Philosophers and statesmen.
His mantra was freedom.
From Selma to Montgomery,
His mantra was freedom.
From Montgomery to Memphis,
His mantra was freedom.
From Birmingham to Cambridge,
His mantra was freedom.

From Accra to Oslo,
His mantra was freedom.
Youngest man to receive the Noble Peace
Prize.
His mantra was freedom.
From Detroit to Da Nang,
His mantra was freedom.
He made it "incandescently clear,"
He opposed an unjust war.
His mantra was freedom.
He called to an age
Where darkness found comfort.
He spoke of light,
Light to guide our feet;
Marching toward justice,
Light to end our suffering,
Moving toward healing,
Light to light our journey,
With shared humanity.
He called on love
To sing a new song.
He called on love
To beat out a new pulse.
He called on love
To send up a new prayer;
A prayer full of the hope
that the past had glimpsed,
A prayer full of the promise
that the day had born,
A prayer full of goodness
constrained by mercy,
That tomorrow will trumpet.
In an age where love is shy,
He led us to our knees in prayer.
He wanted us to love until the sky
glows with grace.
In this time when war is born new

in each hour in our
lives, in our lands,
He prayed that peace finds a perfect place
in our hearts.
He prayed that the words of our mouths
be blessed with
Kindness,
That our songs soar in symphonies
of reconciliation
and healing.
He prayed that our children
see our examples;
He prayed that school doors be opened wide,
Letting all inside.
He prayed that the walls of separation
come down.
(Separate but equal was never equal.)
He spoke from a Birmingham jail.
He prayed and he marched.
He marched ahead of the courts.
He marched ahead of the nation's sentiment.
He marched ahead of the nation's moral tide.
He marched.
We marched.
He marched.
We marched with him.
We marched behind him.
We marched beside him.
He prayed and marched.
We prayed and marched.
And God heard the thundering feet
Of Black mothers
coming up from the sidewalks
Marching to his call.
God heard the tapping feet of young children
Stepping out onto dreams of pride.
God heard the lamentations

of men denied their
Humanity
Marching to his call.
God heard the exhortations
from the pulpits of America.
God heard the exhortations
from the synagogues.
God heard the exhortations
from the mosques,
And the gatherings of people of faith
everywhere,
Echoing his call.
Exhortations!
Citizens of a community of purpose,
Praising the perfect will of our Father,
Committing ourselves to His love,
Committing ourselves to action,
Committing ourselves
To preserve the rich endowment
of God's great earth
For all His peoples.
Echoing his call,
That our cities be havens of joy,
Harbors of harmony;
Echoing his call,
That division be bound,
That misunderstandings dissolve.
Echoing his call,
For clarity over confusion.
Echoing his call.
His voice rang out over the nation.
He went up to the mountaintop,
From the steps of the Lincoln Memorial
Up on the Potomac in Washington -
Amidst two hundred and fifty thousand
foot soldiers
For justice and nonviolence

- who stood with him,
As the nation learned again the meaning of
liberty
And brotherhood and equality;
Those humble masses
still yearning to be free.
He was the advocate for the young
and the old,
Wherever they may be.
He was the advocate for the black,
the brown, the poor,
In America, Africa, Asia and across the seas.
His mule train rehearsed his own martyrdom.
His voice blended with the gospel.
The liturgy was steeped in the tradition
alive in the small Black churches,
As well as the repository of freedom,
the Constitution.
He called for the reserve
that guaranteed the check
Democracy wrote;
Pleaded that weapons of destruction
be replaced
By negotiations of the heart and reason,
That wars cease,
That the silence
of righteous men and women
Be overcome by bold voices for peace,
And that peace breaks out
to claim humanity.
He had a dream.
Deeply rooted in the American dream.
He spoke to freedom everywhere.
He spoke of our shared destiny
as our purest impulse.
He said:
Let us have a new faith,

Deeply rooted in spiritual precept,
A faith shaped by charity,
A faith ratified by unselfish devotion
to family,
A new faith.
With this faith, let us look back
on our dark midnights
And embrace a new, undaunting dawn.
With this faith, let us look back
on centuries of sunsets
And face glorious sunrises.
With this faith, let us look back
on years of noble struggle
And face years of promise still.
With this faith, let us build bridges
of understanding.
With this faith, let us build towers to truth.
With this faith, let men and women,
boys and girls,
Let red and brown and black and white,
Strive for justice, strive for right.
Let a new world arise; let a new day be born.
Let God be pleased with us.
Let God be pleased.

I WILL BE FINE IN THE MORNING_

I don't dance like I used to.
I no longer Boogaloo.
My steps slow drag everywhere.
I'm a broken Ferris wheel at the fair.
My retirement checks are few.
Some old bills are long pass due.
I see more doctors than I want to,
Though I can't remember who.
No matter what my lamentation,
A fresh new day is at my station.
When night rolls up her dying robes,
Retreating from the daylight strobes,
As a new sun is in the dawning,
I'll be fine in the morning.

BOMBAY SPIT

In the time of Idi Amin

Your father,
who they say was from Bombay,
Settled in between
your Ugandan mother's lower lips,
And ample hips,
In exchange for matoke plantain,
waragi liquor,
And a house of her own.
The only home you'd ever known.
He would come
From his sari-ed house bound Indian wife,
Who reeked of curry, to balance his life,
Seeking your mother's dark,
fragrant mystery.
It is a horrible tale of moral history.
Your father went home to India,
Where his bank account went to stay.
He left you
And your three sandy-haired brothers
one day,
Your brothers
with eyes of gray and black faces forlorn,
In the big pink house where you were born.
Which he sold from under you.
(That was the worst that he could do.)
Leaving you homeless and on your own.
He took his sari-ed home bound wife,
He took their three children, too,
Home to India
to his cash stash grown in Uganda
Where he sent it to hide.
Your mother died of damaged pride.
He made his exit so he would not be African

In the land he plundered
and looted with his band.
I pray
He sees your face in choking nightmares
In that far off place
For his disgrace.
May his light brown children be quarrelsome,
His old wife remain mum,
As her children spit on him in his old age.
And he knows your heart's ravaging rage.

*AN OLD BARN*_____

For Betty Sue Rollins-Munroe

I had an old barn
That wasn't worth a darn
But now it's a bistro divine
With a children's aquarium behind
Just a little trick
I pulled out of my bag
To help my mind unwind

OVERSEER OF A DREAM CALLED FREEDOM_____

For Martin Luther King Jr.

From Montage For Martin

He was the overseer of a dream
called freedom
A dream nurtured by the dirt of the land
His fathers helped build
Now planting
now sowing
now plowing
now hoeing
the seed of liberty
liberty refused
liberty denied
liberty impounded
liberty untried
Appointed by the convexion of time
to harvest a dream
not for himself
not for his time
but for all citizens
for all seasons
Though silent the sacred documents
that profess liberty
and still the courts of courage
where liberty's name lay quiet
he encamped about the walls
He stood
Joshua
Seeing the banner of a noble nation
flying freedom abroad
hearing the sound of freedom

championed
but not on our shores
not in darker neighborhoods
he dared
to unfurl justice
to strike the conscience of the nation
unlocking her moral reasoning
impaling bigotry's false pride
putting democracy to the test
His words echoed across a continent
In every town and hamlet
In every hearth and home

THIS IS HOW HE LOVED_____

FOR MARTIN LUTHER KING JR.
FROM MONTAGE FOR MARTIN

This is how he loved.
With a preacher's power
Anointed from above
He trampled through the darkness
And wanted to light the skies with love
Overlooking clenched fist
And hate-filled eyes
Overlooking ghostly white hoods
And damning lies
Though trials and tribulations
Lay in everyway
He found new ground
To build a brighter day
This is how he loved.
He saw the rainbow of humanity
And wanted to make us one
To fling against the darkness
A new and golden sun
Blending Christians and kindred spirits
Blending black and white and brown
Blending young and old
Blending Northern heart and Southern soul
This is how he loved.

He heard the call of the children
In second rate schools
He heard the call of the workers
With second-hand tools
He heard the call
Of those with heavy burdens borne
He heard the call the poor,

the barren, the scorned
He heard the call of those still bound
He heard the call of those passed down
He heard the call of the voiceless
Under a dark days sun
He heard the call of the powerless
He would be their drum
He heard the call down the dark city street
He heard the call down the poor country road
He heard the call of that would not retreat
He heard the call with its bruising load
And he answered
He would lift them
He would lift them high
He would lift their prayers
To a merciful sky

This how he loved.

With a quiet dignity
And a lover's passion
He raised a praise song
Only love could fashion
A praise song
A praise song
A praise song
He would never fail or falter
He raised a praise song upon the altar
He raised a praise song upon
the altar of justice
True believer
True believer
He raised a praise song
A praise song
To place upon the altar of justice
A praise song
A praise song

Ah ra a sha nah, Ah ra a sha nah
A praise song
A praise song
A praise song
With humble majesty
And a martyrs' dread
He saw his own death ahead
And wanted to make it a gift of hope
A gift of pride
This is how he loved
This is how he lived
And this is how he died

EYES TURNED

my heart cried, his eyes turned
soft pain from this wounded man child
whose innocence had fed his narcissism
his short history lay exposed
in the spurious ether
he had been so self deceived
not knowing how long down his life
he must look
to see his reflection
now it seemed betrayed
by his eagerness to be more
than he needed to be
this genius from Africa's registry
the gifts that encase him now
a carved chest commanding his architecture
his waist striding towards
his full endowment
these gifts
were not enough
he became entangled
in a world of quick sand cunning
exposed
to others who will not see
beyond his innocence
his sweetness
not knowing his essence
as I do
not knowing his essence
is unadulterated freshness
he can reclaim today and tomorrow
by looking himself in the heart
and letting
the moving of time
restore that which he lost momentarily
and he will yet be

conqueror
friend
admired
prized
loved
for himself

NOTE ON AN URBAN PRINCE___

The soft eyes of this man child
looks out of a jeweled Mandingo face
brightened by a smile from Heaven.
In flattering hip hop fashion
he looks like a prince
But he has the style that can wear anything.
His short history
speaks of his African registry -
the gifts that encase him now,
a carved chest commanding his architecture,
his waist striding towards his full endowment
will seduce others
who will not know his fast talk
and quick pickup
are the natural play of his innocence
and know his sweet unadulterated essence
as I do.
He can claim today and tomorrow
by looking himself in the heart
and maneuvering
the moving of time
to make himself
conqueror
friend
admired, prized
loved
for himself.
The choice is his,
The prayer is mine.

*I HEAR THE SPIRITS CALL MY NAME*_____

(African Communion)

Memories bejewel my history
testaments
to the brilliance of my early creation
temples to my soul
memories of a million midnights
since the first mother
sang her first lullaby
memories of a million dawns
since the first father
lobbed his net into the sea
memories of night skies
since the first elders
plotted the course of the stars
and wrote our paths in the sacred words
I hear the spirits call my name
I hear the spirits call my name
memories of village circles
where griots sifted history
where the marketplace
knew the price of manhood
and we sang our stories
 in the warm evening
handing them down
from the old ones to the young ones
I hear the spirits call my name
memories of the gathered family
huddled, protecting
generations of rituals
woven into time
with magnificence's simple majesty
the movement of my feet

sings in the movement of my hips
the drum rises from my stomach
to my signifying ear
speaking colors of words
with rich vocabularies
an echoing symphony of my African self
I hear the spirits call my name
My memories dare to talk to God
like the familiar house guest
(God, you know that I know,
that you know)
I hear the spirits call my name
And I wear dark jewels, too
screaming depths of blood and bone
when my children were uprooted
My altar is made of strange wood
broken branches
tossed about the white currents
reaching through the terror
of separation
bearing new fruit in distant lands
invoking again the sap of creation
in dark neighborhoods
down dusky country roads
Memory renews my sassy strut
birthing, building, rapping
humming funky melodies
calling the drum
drums
drum fathers
drum mothers
children of the drum
called back to self
to self, to self
called back to self
I hear the spirits call my name

Now, when I set my table
the spirits speak to me
In consecration of my African soul
When I set my table
I know I am blessed
To be who I am
Who I am, who I am, who I am
I hear the spirits call my name
My name, my name, my name

DON'T YOU THINK I KNOW MY WORTH?

Don't you think I know my worth
Would you have traded gold for me
If I were not worth more than gold
Would you have left your cold palaces
If I were not worth the journey
Would you have twisted
sacred church doctrine
If it weren't for the value of me
I have seen your silos of greed
I have seen your vaults of contraband
I know the price of black bodies
I know the torture of hypocrisy
I know the economy of slavery
I can calculate its cost to the last drop
of blood
You have promised more than you can afford
You have promised to restore
That which you did not possess
You paid the Jew
You paid the Japanese
You paid some of America's first citizens
You fill unmarked boxes in European banks
You bail out the multinationals
You set quotas for the magnates
You subsidize the farmers who will not farm
You arrange handouts for foreign governments
You prop up failing municipalities in the heartland
You bankroll prisons to keep me
off the streets

Your hands have forever emptied my pockets
My paycheck pays your child support
You pretend that my name is welfare

While your family gets jobs
through the back door

Don't you think I know my worth
Don't you know I can count
the staggering cost

I want a refund on my grandfather's death
From labor
I want a credit for my mother's life of poverty
I want a certificate
of deposit for my children's
Unpaid education
I want an investment fund for community
Redevelopment
I want a payday for my underpaid sisters and
Brothers
I want stocks for trading
in my life for your profits
While I hold your soul for collateral

*ONE-EYED PEOPLE*_____

I don't like one eyed people
blinded beyond walls of reason
Too stubborn to want to change
Even when the change is in cash
I don't like one eyed people
half hooked on dumb seasons
Finding justice out of range
Even when the range is all trash

SPOILERS

"An invitation to disaster,"
Said the Monkey to the planet.
"I will see you there," said the Hare,
As they ran along 'side man
With his fiery arrogance
Kicking over anthills,
Stepping on the ants.
"A party for the spoilers,"
Said the underwater crew
Breathing slick pollutants
'til their gills were black and blue.

WHITE PEOPLE

My white colleagues say
to me
"You and I,
black and white
can be
friends."
I
say,
"What's that
you said?"
They repeat.
I
say
"What makes you think
you are white?
you got papers that say
that's right
you got a license
to be white: you know who
your folks were
all the way back
even in the night?
(I smile roundly)
you got a special right
to be white,"
I
ask.
I
don't
take it back
that's why
I'm glad to be black:
they
are
too unsure

to be proud
to be
a bastard
like me,
too unsure
to open
the door
to friendship.

MAN IN POLYESTER SUIT_____
Dedicated to W.E.B. and Robert Mapplethorpe

We cannot stop living
because someone
is afraid
to see us
We cannot zip up
our fly
and refuse to see
because the world
is milk struck
We cannot be invisible
no matter
how many times
we are overlooked
What is the fear
self exposure
self deception (uncovered)
self denial
self hatred
What is the price
alarms
neuroses
stress
exacerbation
blindness
numbness
dumbness
deafness
death
Open my fly
and be relieved
to be human
fallible
failable
Open my fly

and take hold
of your life
 my life
our life
We cannot continue
not knowing
one another.

WHITE NEWSPAPER

Won't find me
in your white newspaper
where you reserve space
based on race
based on wishes
for us
in the obit.
wishing we were dead
on the playgrounds
swinging, giggling, doing headstands
and somersaults
wishing we were children forever
in handcuffs with faces down
wishing we were locked up,
locked out
Never a true shot
of clean souls living clean lives
building our neighborhoods
pillars of our churches
educated and liberated
But we see all the lies
even in the funny sheets
that's why we laugh at the gods
who are so insecure

SONG FOR A YOUNG HERO_____

For Perez Kaino, Kampala, Uganda

My hero's dead
He died young
No more than a soft word
He ran up against bullets
And lost
Before even his prime
He was a son of Africa
Not the Africa of our celebration
But a quarrelsome sick lady
who has distemper
And bad manners
And little regard for young life,
Young heroes
Who have not yet even
Felt their loins tighten
Nor thought grandiose thoughts
But the targets of careless
Adults who have need
Of spanking and discipline
And studies in values
Studies in civilization.
My hero's dead
Cut off from promises
And dreams
That fate may have
provided this son of man
A warm black soul
with ebony moist skin,
rich white teeth
And eyes of clear innocence
Who had only a taste
of gin and was too unburdened
For the corruption of old folk.

73

Shot down before life
Really began
In my Africa
Who forgets herself
And eats her young.
Somewhere between tomorrow
And today
Africa must stop
Living her own funeral.
Africa must stop.
Must stop.
Must stop,
Living her own death.

IS HE BLACK

Is he black?
That's two questions
From the top of his feet
to the crown of his head
He's black
no question
Is he black?
Does he know Egypt?
Does he know Marcus?
Does he know Malcolm?
Does he walk that walk?
And talk that talk
Does he sing his own song?
Does he have a plan for Africa's future?
Word
Black is.

I BE BLACKIN'

Went to a meeting the other day
Thought I'd sold my soul away
Folk there rootin' in Africa's past
Dressed up fine in African sass
Talking the origins of the race
I step right up and take my place
I step right up and chime right in
'Cause I be blackin' with my kin
Said that what we got
Is skin
Made to last with melanin
Said that what we got is "trend"
Setting fashions was always "in"
Said we need to be let in
What we need is discipline
I was blackin' with my kin
When it's over I go home
I go back to my ghetto door
With pimps and junkies
And a one-eyed whore
But for a moment
I was on the mend
'Cause I be blackin' with my kin
'Cause I be blackin' with my kin.

TOTES

Why I totes on my head
Why you wanna know
Why I totes on my head
It's sensible for sho'
My back is straight
My arms are free
Can swat a fly
That's worrying me
Can use my stick
To kill a snake
My hand is straight
my neck is strong
Even got tune
To sing a song.

A ROAD

There's a road that winds
down a-ways
And almost out of sight
I walk that road
Twice a day
At daybreak and at night
The stars keep me company
And labor is my pain
I go to work the white fields
In sunshine and in rain
I know the way to glory
It's down the winding road
I know the way to hell
It's under a heavy load
I carry my share of burdens
I carry my fill of strive
I carry my joy a walking
On the road that carries my life

BAD

Bogeyman gonna git you
if you be bad
Bogeyman gonna git you
if you be bad

Bogeyman,
best friend I ever had.
Bogeyman,
best friend I ever had.

LAST ONE IN SHOULD BRING THE LIGHT

Night's late
Night's dark
Even the dogs
Done stopped their bark
Most everyone sane
Done gone to bed
Nothing much stirring
but the dead
Last one in
should bring the light
No need it to burn
all the night
Light turned low
just a faint glow
So you can see
Around the floor
Light turned low

Wicker damp
Last one in
Should bring the lamp.
Cast a shadow
on the wall
Carry the lamp
down the hall
Quietly go to the room
Move over the bodies
That's playing dumb
Catch the end
of your blanket right
Then quickly
blow out the light
A crack and a cracking

in the bed
Pull the covers
Over your head
Things of the Spirit
Things undead
Let this light
Ward off the dread

PLACE

A man will be a man
A woman knows her place
A child will shine bright
And be quiet as the night
Spoken to for to speak
Otherwise out of sight
An elder is an honor
And a drunk brings a shame
When lunacy strikes
The moon ain't on the wane
But the spirit is possessed
Of family all the same
We feed our holy men
And praise them in His name

*DON DIED TWICE*_____

That girl don died twice
I know she lived before
I saw her at the door
of time
I saw her in my rhyme

DRUM

The intrepid drum beats
in my blood
calling
 home
my children
Fanti
 Ashanti
Bakongo
And Mende
Speaking
tomes
of tones
of soft tongues
indefatigable
indestructible
rooted
 in living
ways
sameness
sung
all the same

WOODEN SOULS

Dedicated to wood sculptor Ulysses Davis

Tree of life
Souls abound
Making men and visions round
The eyes of men
Hands complete
Confounding art of wooden feet
No limits to the open door
The mind in wood
Can really soar
Across the time
Across the seas
On continents unseen, unseen.

RAVENS

a host of ravens
descended on our backyard
bemusing the children
who wanted to know
why this stop on their way
to wherever
I secretly hoped
the truth of the luck
they bring
and that they brought
a special blessing
for my two little ones
who stood wide eyed doing
equations on the why's
of life

WALK WITHOUT SHOES

Are your shoes in the way
of walking, feeling,
knowing the invisible things?
If you can see tomorrow
Why can't you see your way?
If you can enjoy a daydream,
Why can't you enjoy the day?

MAN

Met a man
Sitting on a bench
Who wouldn't give an inch
To me he said
Man is dead
But God is good
I knew
He understood

DEEP OLD MEN

I hear your stories old men.
I hear them with the eyes
in the back of my head.
Your stories make me grow old,
old men.

I see that quiet flash in your eye.
You know I see it because
You did show it to me to see.

I dream in your stories.

I am strong in your tales
of my father, strong warrior,
And rascal, you call him.

Your stories give me grief-
So many sad years in your lives
held close to you
for breath.

I weep in my loins at the sad stories
which years have removed you from the feel,
but already I know memory.
You show me memory in the words
that carry your tales to my ears.

My bellowing laughter rings
from your guts.
I hear myself laugh with stale breath.
Your stories make you speak
memory's words
and laugh memory's laugh.

I grow old, old men, with your tales.

Oh, I see her as she was,

She was love, was she?

You move her love with your feet
in the dirt as you tell of her.
Her hair you see in my eyes
and I hear her move
as you tell your tale.

I will tell this tale to myself
In the day when it is
My tale to tell.

Speak quiet one.

What stories have you?

You have lived these stories too-
Though you are quiet I hear your memory-
It is in your eye, old man.
See me see it there?
I will wait, old one, for your tale.
It will come.

What is it in the shadows?
I see you see it there.
Death.
It chills me.
Will it never come out of the shadows?

I know fear, old men.

You will teach me deeply of fear.
But of shadows I am not afraid;
they walk pass me.

I think I see,
I think I know.

It cannot go away far away;
It must always remain.
You teach me of life,
and shadows,
old men.
I grow deep in your tales.

FAREWELL

For Ulysses Davis, 1913-1990

they kissed his forehead in farewell;
he was already over Egypt,
flying beyond the borders of time
looking out toward Babylon.
they moved in slow earthly sorrow;
he was already over Jordan
soaring above the green valleys.
one by one their hearts were rent,
one by one their songs ceased;
he was already there
out beyond the morning sun
out beyond the evening star

*EVEN THE INNOCENT ARE JUDGED*_____

Not knowing may not
be a capital offense
but it can get you killed:
in a world of high
tech visual literacy
ignorance is poverty
and poverty is replaceable.
misdemeanors of misunderstanding
can get you locked
in a patty wagon
and grilled in a line up.
errors of operation
can get you jailed.
bail is not set
just for the guilty,
the innocent are also judged

*ALL THAT WE OWN*_____

All that we ever own
is memories:
Intangible stock of love
and hate, or warmth,
slights, imprisonments,
Abandon.
We own even death.

And what do we pay
for ownership?
Sometimes the price is light.
We pay with a fond smile,
or a reflection,
or some small, pleasant
unforgotten moment.
Or we may pay
with the heavy weight
of a time betrayed
or kind word unspoken
then no longer worth being said.
Too, we pay with fond and sad
memories of our dead.
And, all that we own is tallied
when we too
become just memories.

OLD PAINT

Generations of life are revealed
in the corners of this old place
as different colors
rainbow
and peel off in festival,
Mirroring our lives.

Layers of our days
spent
Fragments of our souls
hue bent
Reflecting choice and chance
suffered or enjoyed
in layers
Like the colors worn here
and here chipped away.

EPITAPH TO LOVE

If I should die before I love
Let it be known I did not live,
And on my tomb inscribe these words
"Here lies a death that was not had
Because of a love that has not been."

But, if I should love before I die
 Put no tomb about my head,
Let flowers grow
To grace my grave instead.
My grave to grace instead.

CHICK

For Lillie Williams

She sat there on the porch,
an old lady that smelled
of something different
When she held me with love
and a gentleness that was learned
from all the old ladies
she had known all her long life.

She sat there on the porch. Still.
She could not hear.
What was there to hear--
everything she knew--
I could tell by her strong flesh
that I breathed when I snuggled
next to her age.

*I HEAR YOU MARGARET*_____

For Margaret Walker Alexander on the 50th anniversary of
"For My People"

I hear you Margaret
Alibi-ing your consciousness
With confessions of your Southern soul
Africa is south of Europe
Her warmth has bathed the world
In beauty from the bronze age
Until you beckoned the people
To listen to your calculations
Of life in the sunshine

I hear you Margaret
Mocking all your mentors
Serenading souls
With measured hymns
In sly shyness
Then punctuating our present age
With preacher calls
Stumping and shouting
Til the sun goes down

I hear you Margaret
Coyly embracing Europe
And her children in America
In their own language
More fine for your refinement

I hear you Margaret
In the poetry
Of the younger poets,
Building on your century
With word songs of their own,
Made more fertile
By your rivers of words

Your torrents of truth

I hear you Margaret
In the undergrowth of our cities
Humming the memory
Of our dark neighborhoods
Tilling our spiritual connections
Keeping warm our colored folk images
Saving our fabrics for future-kind
To wear in the strut style
That characterizes our sassiness

I hear you Margaret
Savoring the strength
Of womanhood
Testifying to Molly Means and Kissie Lee
Testifying Egypt, Tubman and Bethune
Witnessing Wheatley
With equal relish

I hear you Margaret
Playing a Latin lute on the Mississippi Delta,
In Birmingham and Jackson
Singing of blood and victory
Of men and the promised nation
Scatting in Chicago
Chanting funeral dirges for murdered martyrs
Humming homilies in the labyrinth

I hear you
Coming out of your living
To breathe us the Word
Of our people and their kin
Renewing the long line
Prophesying love
Singing lonely sonnets
Comforting all the people

Lay you down, lay you low now
Margaret
With Langston, and Sterling
And Miles and Martin
Lay you down with the prophets
That you pushed into song
Of a new day
Lay you low, poet and dreamer
Who made your life a poem

MY BROTHER ANTONIO_____

A thank you note to Ieda Santos
(Antonio Castro Alves, March 14, 1847-July 6, 1871. One of
Latin America's greatest poets who wrote about abolition.

My brother Antonio
poet of Brazil
dead before I know you
how could we have spent our days
Singing word songs of Bahian hills
Dancing verbs
Running skies
along Salvador's sensuous coast
Laughing
because we are alive
Because nothing could/can kill us
You are in my clouds
I think you
But I am not sure I can breathe your
brilliance
Feeling free
when I think
You are wrestled back to life
for the beauty of your verses
in the courtyards
under the trees
in lazy libraries where we still find them
Where Dumas speaks
And Pushkin paints
Where Langston tells jokes
You are a mirror to a dark world
That makes us cry
Too soon you are gone from us
Antonio, my young eternal
How did you find your soul
when generations after you forgot liberation
And today they only whisper freedom

Antonio, we are held hostage
in our ignorance
of gourds
and palm wines
and sacred rituals
and gods a plenty
Not only of who we were
but of who we became
are we ignorant
But you, Antonio
you called out our torturers
By name and by number
From all the corners of infamy
Why Antonio
Why
must I discover you anew
in the sweet spicy homage of a scholar
When you so early sang the song of freedom
the song of reclamation
the song of the journey
back through me to you
and on to tomorrow in the anthills of Africa
strolling on the deserts
where cargoes of blood
have been returned to make ash
Hail poet!
Death is uncomfortable in your arms
for I live in you
Now I am witness, Antonio
And the days of my freedom have run cold
The horror, the abominable horror of slavery
the filling, suffocating, nauseating horror
the kidnapping of kingdoms
the transporting of dark human gold
the ghosts of drummers in the sky
over the ocean graves
the suffering mothers

and brain baffled children
warriors stewing in their own slops
this horror you catalogued
walked even more evil ground
in the belly of beasts
building a new monarchy on the shores
of a giant
new island called America
long centuries of suffering rape,
hunger, lynching, inventories of infinite evil
birthin' a god more terrible than the horror
of the slave ship
For it chained the bodies and the minds
Men bowed down to this god
and lost even the pretense of ignorance
Antonio, I vomit its name
but it chokes me
Wait
Hold
for I am struggle
whiteness
There I have it
I am witness
I see
And death shall be too good for this god
who stole the souls of the children
of the horror
eating the white hot parts of their brains
leaving maggots in the tunnels
that housed their eyes
this horror
will devour the whole world
I gather up my weapons
you
and the young ones, students
half dead too
but at my feet I weave miracles of voudon

103

Seeing them remember
through my eyes
what we must do
to call the god to the ground
and crush it under our harden soles
Antonio
bear with me
I am learning leaning on your voice
the voices of a thousand
poets of prophetic light
to save a world

*ON FRIENDSHIP*_____

A friend is the better part of myself
that I dare not lose
He complements me, and
has me see myself as good.

A friend is a future memory
of how I lived my life,
A token of my wealth
that diminishes me
that treasures me.

WHO WOULD SELL A CHILD?____

Who would sell a child
Who would take an infant
Who will sell a child
Into transplant plates
Prolonging fiendish, ghoulish Spirits
Unsaved ones
Who commits these acts
Creatures of the underworld
Satan's sucklings

*THE POET'S SONG*_____

They don't want to hear the poet's song
though they sit there
quietly with smiles.
They don't want to hear the poet's song
because they know of life too,
and they are afraid of the words.
that may make memory come uncalled.
They don't want to hear the poet's song.
No, they don't want to hear the poet's song,
and neither do you.

OLD AGE

What luck
A thousand crow's feet
around my eyes running amuck
My lids droop
and my chin sags
While patches of brown
come to town
Old age visits me

ONLY GOD

Only God can open up the kingdom
Only God controls the skies
God's heaven is infinite space
Only God is really wise

THE HASHISH POEM

far flung Delios, citadel of wind fed freedom
let us abused and weary come
into the womb of your peace
and relax, to fliz from asphalt streets
of ill-bred conformity
and simple delusions
of that man made Gortolanoses
otherwise called society in the annals
of the dead-living
and let us breathe free your airs,
see clearly your browns and greens
and pinks and whites intersealed....

INDIGO LORD

For Askia Mohammed Touré

We learn from you to lift
Our ancient living eyes
Through which we see our sun
Where Kemet never dies.
Your song's throaty majesty is sung
Across African violet skies
For the rebirth, renewal of our strength.

The distant age will see your face
Bearded in the Pharaonic style
Of your elder kin
Who stood upon the Nile
Charting the human course.

We need your voice to lift us
To give us the special Sight.
We need your blessed thunder
For the people of the Light.

KEEP A SMILE

Keep a smile
on your face
And a song
in your heart
And,
way back
in your mind,
Tuck a good laugh
from a happy time.

Carry no anger
from one yard
to the next.

LAMENT ON LINCOLN STREET'S PASSING

This old city street
is from the time when city streets
were country
And people passed a tippin' their hats
and howdy doing,
Cutting gracious paths
through old ladies' backyards
with a 'cuse me ma'am
and an if'n you please.

There were trees so shady, then,
and shutters white, or greenest green,
And everybody knew everybody
("You James' son ain't you" or
"Ain't you Vi's little girl?")

Now this street is slowly passing.
Old homes ain't there with their charm
and memories
anymore,
And some folks speak
while some folks don't
And some don't even know yo' name.
There's new buildings coming up
with red brick that bites the eye,
and shocks old houses
that blush in their quiet color frames-
But there are still some things
that remain
like the dip in the street
and the white washed house
on the corner (now),
And folks who could ne'er call home

any other name
than Lincoln Street.

ONE TRAIN GOES THROUGH TOWN

One train goes through town
One train on only one track
And when you've almost forgotten it's there
It goes clack, clack, clack
WOO-OOO-OOO-OOO-OOO
And you remember
One train goes through town
One train on only one track.

*THE FACULTY MEETING*_____

Pose,
posture,
gesture,
Motion carried.

ADOPTION

A child deserves a life
home spirit, Jell-O and hugs
balance and sanity
health and happiness
A child deserves a life
full and free
wherever there is love

*REACHING FOR THE KEYS*___

For Sister Curley Powell

As long as she could play
those keys
She made music day and night
As long as she could play
those keys
She played with pure delight
As long as she could play
she was reaching for the keys
And somewhere out of sight
of mortals
a piano still is tuned
a chord echoes bright
As she plays those keys just right
a choir is rising up
an organ glides right in
As the gospel songs begin
and the bass line trembles
and some saints are on their knees
Somewhere she is smiling
somewhere she is pleased
as she reaches for the keys.

MY FACE IS ON FIRE

My face is on fire
He's over there laughing
He's telling his boy friend
about how Mama has forgotten
something again
Does he know how many things
you have to remember
Does he know how many times
you wash his underwear
Does he know how many battlefields
of logistics
it takes you
To keep his happy face laughing
Does he know the man hours
you clock
on his behalf
Does he know his world is hinged
 to your casual existence
Tell him, Mama, so his sons
and daughters won't inherit
his foolishness
Tell him, Mama, how many nights
you keep the lights on
in heaven
(So he can laugh)
Tell him who you are, Mama
He does not know
Maybe he had better ask
somebody

CARTAGENA

Cartagena
lady eternal
singing your Caribe
standing full breasted queen
of indecipherable age
beauty
Sharing your warm heart
with countless lovers
and friends
Cartagena
lady magical mystical nights
of afro-latin rhythms
and days of boats garlanded
in your Spanish hair
singing your Caribe
with Indian charm
Cartagena
sun mother
with emerald eyes
blushing morning
seizing hearts
with Caribe lullabies
Cartagena
woman of the Indies

GENIUS, YES

It is difficult
to be a genius
among people
whose talents
are more narrow.
My psychiatrist
advised
but I
devised
a plan
of my very own.
I now just
laugh
and smile
at life
and leave
most things
alone.

CAMPING

We
slept
slept
Slept
SLEPT
SLEPT TOGETHER
in sun and in rain

We
slept
slept
slept
slept
Slept Together
Look
look
look
Look
how the sun
cooked our brains
how the sun
cooked our brains

We
slept
slept
slept
SLEPT
SLEPT TOGETHER
under roofs
and in drains
SEE
see
see
SEE

how the rain
washed our stains
how the rain
washed our stains

We
slept

slept
slept
SLEPT
SLEPT TOGETHER
in cool winter rains
Look
look
look
Look
how the wind
left us drained
how the wind
left us drained

TIMES

There are times
There are reasons
There are rhymes
There are seasons

But I can't find anything
That explains why
You used my love on me

My love couldn't hold you
So you got me good
You did all the things
A bad girl could
You used my love on me

SO YOU WANT TO BE A JACKSON_

So you want to be a
Jackson
With stardom
Every day
With noses
Just alike
Cupid animals
at play
Well you had better
Just be thankful
For the person that you are
You had better
Just be thankful
Cause you're better
As you are.

YOU CAME TO HEAR ME POET__

So you came to hear me poet
So you came to hear me play
So you came to sing with me
To see what we can say

So you came with open minds
So you came with minds made up
And I came to say the truth
 And jam it up your butts

So I came to rock your castles
And to throw out all your lies
I came to blow a trumpet
And open up your skies

I came to sing your songs
To massage your waking dreams
I came to make you laugh at life
And all its sagging seams

I love to be the poet
Nothing less, nothing more
So I hope you came to hear me
To open up the door

*JUST THE WAY*_____

It is just the way
You pain your face
To hear the pain
In my poem

It is just the way
You smile your eyes
To hear the laughter
In my song

It is just the way
You feel my heart
In the heartbeat
Of my joy
That tells me
That you love me

ACCIDENT

It all boils down to an accident
making you aware of your vulnerability
And the split second between
life and death.
As if broken headlights or smashed doors
matter in comparison
how about the critical appointment
that you could not keep anyway
'Cause another vehicle was sent
hurling into your psychospace
And redesigning your nose
unceremoniously and without regret
Simple to suggest that you could/should
have been doing other things
Or not going out, not turning left
or right, not driving
Or not making a rendezvous
Not being anywhere near there
or simply not being born
Simple to suggest that you could have
avoided life
pain
stress
duress

ALL THE THINGS WE ARE_____

All the things we are
chocolate hypertension
greasy sluggishness
sugar coated
bloated
black burned lungs
mucous membranes of excess starch
carbonated gases of addictive sodas
and acid tonics
All the things we are
come in by our mouths
over which our brains
have lost control

EMPTY BOX

She has a little box
that no one ever wanted
for very long
so she turned into a sour face
And spat out forgeries of
half truths
with poisoned tips of feigned intimacy
So that certain pain was inevitable
It was a small price to pay
for coming spinsterhood
And unfulfilled moments from girlhood
She is not rare
Her sisters are the unloved rejects
of romance
Less fortunate because less loving
Empty boxes without promise

BRAND NAMES

Commercial message
Get up
Check on your kitchen sink
Is this Joy or Ivory
It's got to make you think
Are the ingredients the same
Are the chemicals labeled plain
Could the rising agent spoil
before the date expires
Is the color fashion ready
Or has the new vogue not arrived
Check the label in your suit
Was it made in Hong Kong
Is that shirt a silk or cotton
Would the blend fade
If washed too warm
or are the name brands
a bunch of stuff
Put out to make you
buy
Get up
Check your kitchen sink
It's much more than you think

BURN THE BOX

this pantheon of mindlessness
perched on a generation
of unfed brains
protein deficient
bombarded by misshapen
images of magic and glitter
violent cartoons
white gods or girls
in business suits or steel hats
all deified
or pearl lace twirls
remakes of junky Judy Garland/
her non-singing daughter
Tammy Faye Minnelli
mixed with smells of stale poverty
that you can get use to
if you have to
you don't know the difference
you don't know
you don't smell it
Busting out alarm to Dove users
this shock treatment
of commercials
telling you, steal, rob
smoke, pollute
never knowing your head is wired

you wonder why
sirens are always in your neighborhood
on and off the box
remote control
it does not bother you
America the beautiful
has severed your soul
severed your connection

with humanity
paid TV is a nightmare
from which no one will awaken

I PLAYED GAMES

I played cowboys and Indians
and waxed my red bicycle
'til I could see my long face in it.
I sat on steps and talked
'til I was called home
or no one else would be left
if I did not go when the last one was called.
I played checkers and bull's eye
with my huggie that I stole.
I played cops and robbers,
rode my bicycle, and twirled my lasso
to catch the imaginary bull.
I played cards and caddied
for old men with money.
I bought records and we listened to them
at everybody's house.
I chipped in to buy cigarettes
so we could smoke in fear of getting caught.
I played games of all kinds--
I played horseshoes and eight ball--
I played games I don't remember.
I played.
I played cowboys and Indians.
And then I learned to do the do.

*YOU ARE TWO PEOPLE*_____

You are two people
Neither of which I know very well
Not as well
At any rate
As I thought I knew
The one of you

But let me tell
The two of you
That the two of us
Are through

*WHEN LADIES WHISTLE*_____

God doesn't like it
When ladies whistle
The whole heaven heaves
Under the shrill tones
That shatters the governments
Of men and question the order
Of the universe
Is relativity a genderless equation
Do the myths protect the producers
Of the myths
But not their sisters
Or mothers

JAZZ

The sound grows
deepens
a musical commune
of self love, other love
feeling
hearing
using the first impulse
of the universe
sounds
setting free the conjuring
soul
a new sound leads
following a side path
to a new harmony
one by one
all with all
a different drummer
takes flight
in a sustained sky
over Congo
rich and varied
polyrhythmic heart
lush
shrill
deep
dark
funky
earthy
exhilarating
symbol and sun
jazz

MEASURE

The grave is no measure
of the man
It is a mere passing place.
We are all
graveyard sons
and daughters
Sent to the slaughter
by our sins

SLIDE

Slide brother slide
Dip brother
Slide
Hip
Jive
Slide brother slide.
Walk your walk
Across this planet
Slide brother
Slide

SHE IS THE SOURCE

See how she can strut--
would put another to shame.
She is black and shines light silver
on her moist ebony skin;
she is a queen
No need to say she is loud,
does not a queen own
the very sound she makes.
The millennia have made her
strong and wise and wicked
and shy and all else.
The rain forest has made her quick.
The desert has bronzed her
time and time and time again.
The land has fed her wisdom.
She sees with the eyes of her mothers.
Her reign is eternal.
She is the source.

KNOWING

First you got to know that
You know that you are Black
Then you can know that
You know that you are white
And red and yellow too
Then, you can know that you are
Black

GORÉE

They must gather at Gorée.
One from each tribe of Africa.
One from each place in the outer lands
Where we have grown.
Let the drum be
long and dark, somber.
Wailing.
Let us gather at Gorée
for the cleansing
At the cross of the hunters,
looters, liars,
Gather them here in effigy.
Let the music begin.
As the day sees its end.
Cast out the night wings,
the tormented souls
the ancestral agonies
hovering over the place.
Let the cleansing have one voice,
continuous, piercing, purging,
Purifying.
Let the waters settle
like libations to living memory
Let the world be cleansed
of the great sin.
Stop the moment forever
in our minds.
Rise up. Rise up. Nation.
Gorée

NECKBONES

Neckbones, pigtails, and chicken feet,
We got the food others wouldn't eat.
We added love,
And beans and rice,
Made them delicacies,
Made them nice.
Now, at the store they charge more,
For what was once thrown out the door.
They steal our muscles,
(For their cultural Olympics)
And pawn our music,
Recognizing our genius, later
When some imitator
Forgets or brags about
Where he got his second hand
Straight-from-the-black blues.
The prisons are filled
With my people.
The schools are imprisoning our minds,
Crushing Black children's wills,
While science neglects our ills.
Can't get a piece of the action,
Can't get a piece of the pie.
We are not in on the take,
No matter how much we make.

My brothers want jobs,
Not handouts.
My mother wants peace
For her sons and daughters
So she can die loving America.
My children want schools and tools,
And fun and joy-not hate.
My father and I want justice
With her eyes wide open

And her head on straight.

Can't they see.
Can't they see
That freedom ain't free
Unless it's you and me
Both free?
Let freedom ring,
We sing, still.
Let freedom ring, America!

THE DEATH OF JESSE JACKSON_

If you live big, better die big
Or people'll talk about you. Know
What I'm saying. Like
Ain't that nothing. Died in his sleep.
Choked to death in a Jewish restaurant
Slipped in the men's room in Macy's,
Fractured his skull. Bled to death before
They could get the third floor elevator
unstuck.
Better be shot, staved, bombed or poisoned
If you die young, Better
Provide gruesome death details
for investigative
Reporters if you die young.
Definitely unhistoric,
Devoid of drama, if your plane goes down
Over nowhere that we can pronounce, or for
Which there is no street name
In our neighborhood.
And if you die old, better die running,
Running scared, running for office,
running for cover
Running 'cause you ain't supposed to die
a natural death
Better have three heads
 that nobody's figured out
Anchorman says
"Inside this head is a brain….
Inside this head is …. Damn if we know …"
Field day for instant analysts
Called forth for mini-blinks on the tube.
If you die old you'd be advised
To have no cash unless it's a stash
Of 1,000 thousand dollar bills in an alligator
Box in the back of an old Motorola.

If you die old better have three strikes
Against you. Strike one, Bucked the system.
Strike two. Embraced the peace.
Strike three.
The FBI can't release their records
Until you're stone gone dead.
Ain't supposed to die if you're Jesse Jackson.
Michael is exempt. He'll probably write
A hit groove to be beamed from space
Every one hundred years on the anniversary
Of his demise. And Diana
who never could sing anyway,
won't show up for the funeral.
Ain't suppose to die a natural death.
If you live big, better die big.

RAP DANCE

The rhythms rap the music
sending hip hop thru the air
pounding primordial pulses
unchaining sun children
feeling free
(for a little while)
defying gravity
sustained by foreverwhile memory
Turntable generation
zapping your African bodies
across centuries
Claiming,
always claiming
your natural self
unspoiled man and woman
unspoiled line
forever purifying with your soul
Dance
jump, shout, call
Scream rhythms
the message of moment-ness
unmolested
mothered by the drums
(it's in the music)

boom, boom, boom
clap clap, clap clap, clap clap clap clap,
go ahead
tambourine band
drum bodies
fast feet flee, fly
slide
frenzy
Ho
Somebody scream

147

Dance to the sister
dance to the brother
dance to the sun
dance to the night
dance to the dawn
Rock, hammer, hammer
sending bad, bad
rhythms to the universal soul
sending bad, bad
Search the sen---sation
rap generation
rhythm nation
warrior dancers
wonder dancers
cosmic pulse—sation

Somebody say ho
say, say, say, ho
riot rhythms
pillow base smooth, slowing it down
slow, slow, slow, slow it down
down, down
not afraid for souls to touch
arms around strong necks
arms around sweet happy hips
Dance like you just don't care
Rhythm nation
rap generation.
You got it going on

RED HEAD HARPIST _____

A red head harpist on a horse
in my dreams did appear
What she did with all my thoughts
Cannot be measured here.
A violent life, a violent death
was the promise of this quest
but I did woo the read head harpist
who did sit upon my chest;
Such a dread flirtation, yet, which
my spirit did not resist.
I gave my stove a new invention,
it fried my brain and drained my head.
I gave my friends a new condition,
they stole my cash and took my plane.
I gave my love a new dimension,
she sold her soul out in the rain.
I gave clock a leave of absence,
it gave my life a loose refrain
I gave my family grief at night,
I gave them pain, I gave them fright.
The leaves of grass and snow powder kill;
they once were used to cure man's ills.
Now a nightmare of cold retreat
making ghosts on dead end streets.
And from this grave my curses yell,
I rode that beat, I rode to hell
I rode that red head harpist's horse
I rode that dreadful street and lost.

BACK

The whole world knows when
you are turning over on this
old screechy bed.
Was it something that I did?
Was it something that I said
that made you turn your back on me?
Is it that I have not conquered cities
on your behalf
or laid diamonds at your feet?
Forgive me, my sweet.
Are there other thoughts more
precious than the pillow on which I lay
my head to occupy your reason?
Can it be it's time to turn
from now to another season?
What advice does your shoulder give
as you give me your back?
Is it something that I did?
Is it something that I lack?

*SURVIVOR'S CREED*_____

They may distort my history
And deny my heritage
They may poison my fields
And trick my brothers
They may bend my back
And call my children names
They may buy my leaders
And sell my dreams
They may send my sons to war
And steal my food
But will all my strength
I shall hold on
For I have steeled my mind
And nothing shall separate
Me from myself.

THE DAYS OF MY FREEDOM
HAVE RUN COLD_____
(or Runaway Slave)
For actor, Joseph Mydell, morning, July, 1989

Tarred and feathered, whipped and drawn,
Darn near lynched, been all
Run with every breath that's in me
Sailing on freedom's shifting seas
No 'seer of darkness could catch me
No gunner could shoot me back, entrapped
'Been determined as an eel to keep me loose
Watering holes done been poisoned
Winds been sniffed by hell's canines.
Nothing but nothing can hold me.
I've had a dream of capture,
Like shackles 'round my papa and mama
Kings and queens of forgotten days;
Like shackles 'round my seedlings
Princes of the earth shadowed from shining
In their full sun's majesty;
Like the glory of the ages
now bereft of hero's deed's
Like all my history shredded in chips
Of worthless ash burned and weighted down.
Yet, when my ears swoon
with coward's callings
Of son's gone from their dark heritages,
Or, sisters sneaking
away from the self known tree.

When I hear retold my journey's flight
As though it were a lie to posterity,
When I see the sickness of cowards' play
In my children's children's deeds;
When I see betrayed my toil and cunning,

My breathless escapes and daring raids,
The days of my freedom run cold.
I ask for hell but am refused.
I ask for death but am rejected.
There is no way I can stop running
Or, rest my heaven bound ride
'til you run with me, strongly,
Through the winds of our deliverance
Race in freedom's wind, stride unbroken,

ETHIOPIA

Wine and new wine, twins on which
some have built modern civilization
have not dulled my memory.
What moments of monuments erected
to your living presence.

Time is not finished with you, Ethiopia.
Was I quiet when you built Egypt?
Was I quiet when you sang me a lullaby
for a thousand years?
Was I quiet when you took your case to
humanity, unembraced?
Was I quiet when the wasting
famine seized your children's bellies?
Was I ever quiet? Was I quiet
When you forbade me to moan?
Was I quiet when
Lies were told about your chastity?
Was I shut up
when it was said you were not the
mother of Christ,
and the grandmother of the holy rites?

I shall never be quiet as long as men call
you whore and I know
you are the vessel of life.
I have forgiven nothing
that has been done to you.

BLUES LAYER____

Hey, Mr. Blues Player,
Play me a love song
and make it hurt way down deep
in the deserted streets where blues
come to play.
Hey, Mr. Blues Player,
Play me a mood song which moans
and flirts up on abandoned bridges
where blues go to stay.
Make it holler in a voice forlorn
Make it rift in a sound near gone
Make it wallow in the pains of love,
coming home in a righteous groan
Play me the blues
like B.B. or Bessie. Play me a love song
with a bible belt beat. Play me a love song
 and make it hurt real sweet.

ANGELS WITH WHITE FACES____

Angels with white faces always
hell scaring
pink faced monsters with cherub smiles
cunningly designed to get under my psyche
and steal my soul
to sell in some far off fantasy freak land
called heaven
Puffed up on clouds of deceit
I keep one trusty eye
on the angels
and the nuns
and the priests
and the bishops
and the pope
and Billy Graham
and Fulton Sheen
and all the pink faced soul suckers on t.v.
out to pollute God
Grabbing the white pink heads
in my brain, recycling them
in cool brown color
with id's from my neighborhood

ALL BLACKS ARE AFRICANS_____

All Blacks are Africans
Whether they know it or not
Some are ignorant of their birthright,
Some are ashamed,
Some suffer from estrangement
and others claim no name.
But, Africa knows her children.
She waits
while memory comes home.

*MARY OF THE SADNESS*_____

I know your check bounced again
and it is past time for
your period and you have nothing
to wear to church which
never ends
and you've had to skip Christmas
and Easter frocks and frills
and Halloween frightens you
and there is nothing but fake
revolutionary brothers
who talk about truth and understanding
and misunderstand your womanhood
and pretty sexy plastic men who interest
you briefly only briefly and your baby is sick
with future hypertension and racial stress
and the books you read
are never about you or yours
and eternity
seems to be
a place where God hides
with perhaps some divine joke
to tell and your feet hurt
and the children sass and
it's time for a new idea
not another beer and you're
too tired too tired too tired
so you take a little sadness
and day "f' it and do
what you will to get by and buy
a little joy, take a little sadness.

PICTURE, PICTURE PAINTED___

Picture, picture painted
One white with long auburn hair
And blue eyes in pious stare
Sits in place
Attended by the twelve
--one who would betray
Picture, picture painted
All now sainted—save the two
May all be true
If you believe
But the colors of the skins
Do deceive
If our history
Is right black or brown the skin
Not white
Picture, picture, paint

POETS ARE PRECIOUS PEOPLE__

I cannot read your poetry
anymore
because it does not sing or dance
it's like a fat lady in a cluttered front room
it puts on airs
and crowds whatnots everywhere.
I cannot read your poetry either
it pretends its waters are deep
but there is not beach
to make my feet feel the sands of reason.
And your poetry
yells and curses
without purpose,
missing the essential rhythms of real talk.
I'd rather listen to Sonia who knows
what she sees
and says it with a special vision.

GARDENS OF STONE

Dedicated to the victims AIDS

Where once joy and sunshine brightly shone
Where love and laughter would adorn
Stand now their graves in garden stone
Remembering wretched souls in bodies worn,
What manner of sin has been unleashed
To end such passionate men,
And women,
That never mattered more till now
And never more in youth.
I wholly pray a quick return
To a more sane use of science
In whose oath of life we find
No more dread abuse than the rocks
That grow by the hour
In this grave of stone.
When God's final measure is lost
Will his sons atone
For their lapse of memory
On every hand
For man's inhumanity to man.

TIE

Tie around my neck
Dangling like some symbol
of enslavement
    to European cultural connections.
Even when it dangles in my salad (mixed)
    or drags through my butter (melted)
It has this mystic power over me
    to make me look ridiculously
    unfree.
For a moment the more comfortable
    dashiki was in vogue
    (during the days of I'm black
and I'm proud)
    Then J.C. Penny mass produced it
    leaving my culture
and consciousness defiled.
Though I now rap a kente with
    cheap leather trim (mocking my Africa)
    And wear desecratingly
wrong colors medallions
    supposedly symbolic of the blood,
the land,
the people
I know soon I will go Euro-mad again
    And tie this tie around my neck
Because it reminds me
that I want to be a slave
choked up in a world that does
not want to feel
choked off from a world that does
not want to know
me
My tie, myself and I
sedated

And my tie matching my overhard shoes,
my unnecessary lapels
my meaningless button down shirt
my useless suit pockets etc., etc.
None of which gives me comfort
Though it all gives me access
to a tie world that chokes me
chokes me
chokes me
even down to my too tight jockey shorts.
Hello.

BEING BLACK
*IN MY NEIGHBORHOOD*_____

Being Black in my neighborhood
Is a splendid thing
Like bright sunshine
And new clothes in Spring.
We got our own special ways
And our own special days.
Like Sunday morning.
Now that's a time
For colored boys and girls
To put on clothes as they say
And pose and strut,
Boys in their three piece suits,
Clean,
Know what I mean,
And girls so shiny
Hair greased back, with pretty curls
And bows and braids.
Ah, the whole neighborhood
Is laid.
Use to even be hats
And white patent leather pocketbooks
For handkerchiefs only.
Being Black in my neighborhood
Is a splendid thing,
Like singing in the Summer
On the corner
Under the moth encircled
Lamppost.
Oh, what joy it is
on my block
Being Black.

LAMENT ON LINCOLN STREET'S PASSING

This old city street
is from the time when city streets
were country
And people passed a tippin' their hats
and howdy doin',
Cutting gracious paths
through old ladies' backyards
with a 'cuse me ma'am
and an if'n you please.

There were trees so shady, then, and shutters white, or
greenest green,
And everybody knew everybody
("You James son ain't you" or
"Ain't you Vi's little girl?)

Now this street is slowly passing,
Old homes ain't there with their charm
and memories
anymore,
And some folks speak
while some folks don't
And some don't even know yo' name.

There's new building coming up
with red brick that bites the eye,
and shocks old houses
that blush in their quiet color frames
But there are still some things
that remain
like the dip in the street
and the white washed house

165

on the corner (now),
And folks who could ne'er call home
any other name
than Lincoln Street.

.

GLAD LADIES

Lord, these Glad ladies
sat
mighty
pretty
in full color, in full spirit
in the second pew,
pouring forth Jesus-ness joy
of jubilee.
Sanctified,
sweatless in ecstasy
of revival.
Coming up, Lord
to their feet
one by one
Shouting
the fire dance.
Blue pill box hatted lady
all matching everything
blue glow
next to Sister all fire red
side
that fine powdered perfectly pretty
middle life lady
in brown.
Positioned
threesome
Knowing their eye catching beauty,
Not to be outdone in the holy ghost.
Waiting respectfully their turn:
One by one
they shout
O' these Glad ladies
In command of the temple:
God is glad. Hallelujah!

THE OLE NEIGHBORHOOD_____

going back there now
is to see it in the dark hollow eyes
of ex-friends long since dead
from gangster toxins
that stole their brains
and swallowed up their dreams.

what lethal substances
in a world of primordial innocence,
a world that cannot write too well anyway.

memories witness our childhood
surprised at growing up
finding a synthetic world
challenging us to be a part of the rainbow,
demanding we be multi-intellectual.
memories
borne of the old neighborhood
where only ghosts live.
a hundred atom bombs
should visit
the drug pushers
downtown and on the high seas
with wall street connections
and government subsidies.

*TRUTHFEASTING*_____

For Nathaniel Bracey

Even when it hurts
go about sharing
and being the people's distant eyes
or whatever they need
cause
We will never be free
unless our minds are free,
We will never be strong
unless weakness is taboo
We will never be us
until we cease being others
And what we know
grows
as truthfeasting

MOST OF MY LIFE

Dedicated to the Memory of Langston Hughes

Most of my life
has been spent moving
from Bakersfield to Baltimore,
though Harlem is my home.

Most of my life
has been spent traveling,
sometimes weary, sometimes sad
from Moscow to Ashkhabad.

Most of my life
has been spent singing "a dramatic song"
telling a story—of times and hearts betrayed
and tambourines to glory;

And dancing,
hour by hour,
in phantom lands like Dixie
pulling Jim Crow's plow.

Most of my life
has been spent knowing people,
touching them and holding fast,
sharing hopes for their future;
distilling in their past.

Most of my life
has been spent in wonder and wandering
through America's promise,
with curses unsaid,
with tickets returned and a mailbox
for the dead.

Most of my life
has been spent with a poet's song
and plays for thoughts to roam.
And, now, all of my life has been spent,
America.
Still, Harlem is my home.

.

RAISIN' UP

Mama really cared.
And we never dared
Act up in public
Pout or frown,
At least when mama was around.
We said "yes ma'am" and "yes sir"
And never said a bad word
We were proud, never loud
And we didn't sass back
To older folks who were Black.

And Daddy was just as strong.
Quiet.
Though nothing much said
He backed Mama's every word

PIG LATIN

What language asked the sister
 from Africa
Do you speak at home
I mean, when you are alone
With your family
I see, I said
Remembering my family tree
Knowing we ain't free
"it a is a ig pa
at in lay", I say

BLACK ON BLACK

Hey, ole Cotton,
I just got back
From up in the city
Where it's Black on Black;
Homicide, genocide
Robbery, rape—
Death in alleyways
Terror on the reign;
Blacks killing Blacks
Like they're going insane.

Whoa, ole Cotton,
It's not just the city.
To tell you the truth
I'm scared to be back.
It's here too
killing Black on Black.
Sociologists, psychologists
And politicians,
They can't agree;
We are killing
Each other, but yet
They can't see
It is not the pressures
Of poverty.
We've always been poor.
I'm not going to buy
That jive anymore
Mothers without children,
Fathers without bail,
Mere children sent to jail;
Slugging and mugging
And robbery and rape.

174

Husbands and wives dead
'Cause of something they said.
And bullets in the heads
Of brothers, mothers, sisters and sons.
Saturday night specials;
Homes with guns.

When will it end,
This spilling of blood?
When will it end,
This killing of men?
When will it end,
When?

WE HAVE BEEN AT SCHOOL ALL DAY

We have been at school all day
And have not heard the bell.
We have been at school all day
And still our lives are hell.

Maybe,
The promise of the dream
"Education to set us free"
Was never meant to be
Reality.

Our hopes
Were set upon a sea
Of never ending toil
And the lesson learned
Is that we will never be free
If someone lets us be

PROLOGUE

A shade of darkness covers us
We who put in God our trust
We of the ancient Black race of He
We who want only to be free

*FOURTH OF JULY*_____

Fourth of July
And brothers and sisters
Celebrating
The way they know how
With cookouts
And barbecues
And people hugging people
And drinking beer
And drinking wine
And telling lies
--And telling lies
And laughing.
Red, white and blue
And fire
Crackers nowhere
Playing chess
With shiny faces
And sounds of jazz
Filling spaces.
Fourth of July
And brothers and sisters
celebrating
The way they know how.

SEE THAT BROTHER THERE____

See that brother there
traveling light
playing in the snow
on this sun shiny day
making Mother Africa
ashamed of making him Black
in the hot coals of her ancient
bosom
Can't respect his mama
cause he chose not to choose her
for the mother-wife-woman image
for posterity
Curse his children
stone them
or tie them to hamburger stands
and paint "for whites only"
On signs around their necks
or let their blood
drain from them
for their father's sin
against Ham
against Sheba
against his life force
Let his curse
fall on his family's family
time unfolding.

Does he know the magnitude
of his sin?
Tell him
before he brings
down the night
about his ancestors
in shame

Tell the brother
So he can know
Hell comes
from playing in the snow.

SOLEDAD LADY

Lady
swaying your hips
walking your caribe
with magical, mystical
afrolatin liquid rhythms
you are the queen of the Indies..

I CAN'T HEAR NOBODY SINGING

Sun goes down much too quick
Daylight's eye harsh and plain
I can't hear nobody singing
I'm crying the blues again
Crying for my brother
Who's lost his own
Crying for the babies
Who's lost faint light
Crying for the people
Of the night
Gonna get strong
And stop these tears
Gonna get wise
And shake my fears
Gonna get right
You will see
Gonna set right
As a family
Daylight's eye harsh and plain
I can't hear nobody singing
And I'm crying the blues again

BLACK COLLEGE KILLING FIELD

Killing a Black college today.
By letting whites who would not
otherwise be hired anywhere else
infiltrate the infrastructure
and run covert operations
while home grown and imported
coloreds whose sincerest desire
is to be, become, remain
uncle Toms, Dr. Toms and Aunt Janes
apologize for their ancestry
walk on their history and
kiss the butts of the white niggers
Killing a Black college today.
By dumping on those who believe
in the greatness of blackness,
stampeding our strong voices.
White nigger, black nigger,
black nigger, white nigger.
Killing a Black college today.

TECHNOGLYPS

The wind whistles through the open windows
of abandoned cars. Signs
etched in techno waste
recall our transport across these plains—
first on foot, then on steed,
then on roaring giants of steel and fiberglass.
Deserted monuments
rise up as symbols of our longing
to defy gravity. But graves are not free
of the binding force of this place
Whose breath we contaminated.
The admonition, "Don't eat anything
that glows in the dark," is lost now
as the neon-like playground of our folly
begins to dance at dusk.

*MORNING'S COMING SOON*____

Morning's coming soon
and I shall cast off this
sleepy lethargy
and a trillion sparks of energy
will possess me.
I shall be a day person.

PLACE OF THE OTHER'S SEE ___
City of the Angel's Watch

I was there three thousand years and more
When then I was called
The Place of the Other's See.
I was there midst air and stone
And kept my winds close to me
I was there when men came
to name me names that
Speak to them of my presence.
David was but one my shadow followed
Though more remembered he than others.
I made the mountains green
and high
Then bid them turn to stone
and sand;
And will level them to valley.
I was the blood and voice of prophets,
The message in law and change.
I have swept the fields and fields of battle
And writ the names of my guests in
the earth and stone.
I was the path and way of Jesus,
And I shall know the last of days,
Changing the sky in quickly force
And turning a light to earth unseen before.
I am called the Place of the Other's See,
I am called many names and shall be,
I am Jerusalem.

FASHION A NEW WORLD

Fashion a new world, Lord
boundless and bright
Where ignorance subsides
And burdens are light

Set a new table, Lord
full for the feast
Let us all sit together, Lord
Let all hunger cease

Build a new temple, Lord
safe and secure
sheltering the lost
In thee we endure

Make a new world, Lord
joyous and right
where justice and mercy
keep watch through the night

MANDY LO'

Don't wake the man too soon, Mandy Lo'
Don't wake the man too soon,
'Cause when he sleeps his spirit flies
While here his body lies.
Don't wake the man too soon.
Don't wake the man too soon

IN PASSING

For Charles Flax and Roland Carter

Two men meeting
along life's path
One wearing greatness
without the hearing
The other who hath
it yet to wear

In the passing
of the evening
One teaches all
before his leaving
The other grows older
for on his shoulder
The mantle falls

The mantle of the good great man
that mantle moves
From man to man
for it is a measure
Of all men
world without end

THE HEMORRHOIDAL SMILE___

I know you've seen
the hemorrhoidal smile
And seen it more than twice
on principals
and teachers
bent on looking stern
And policemen
who refuse to be nice
The uncomfortable
(I'm not giving in)
(And don't you dare breathe)
Smile
With teeth sealed tight,
mouth puffed out
And sometimes accompanied
by a constipated pout.
You know you've seen it.

BURY ME NOT

Bury me not
While I am still breathing life
Cutting through traffic
Fighting against white currents

Stumbling
down blind alleyways
Stirring a new brew
For the new day's sun

Bury me not
While I yet dream
While music still plays
In my glad ears
And my ancestors
Keep me company by day

Bury me not
While I am yet alive

HARMONY

Now take me,
I laugh at bigots
Who pout and frown,
Faces all screwed up,
Like bulldogs or hounds,
Or uppity folks that
Don't like this or that,
Or you or me.
They ain't free.
You see,
Their prejudices keep them in chains.
In some places,
Some people
Walk on the other side of the street,
To keep out of the shadow
Of their brothers.
Let them walk wherever
They will.
They can't get off the world.
And imagine;
Segregated cemeteries,
For dogs and cats.
Dig that for in-hu-man-i-ty.
Can't they see,
Ain't nobody free,
Unless we are all free.

SOMETIME LIES

There are sometime lies
told sometimes
carelessly
callously
midnight lies
private lies
political lies
Lies
Ready or not
lies hurt
lies kill.

193

*EMANCIPATION OCCASION*_____

A cry of joy, of jubilee,
Rang loud from souls enslaved
And orators with rich voices raised
Eloquently sang Lincoln's praise.

A hundred days said he
For rebel armies to disband
Restore peace to the land,
Or, he'd let the slaves go free.

From September to January's first day
The stage was set so bold,
Though much life and blood were spent.
The day came without the South's consent.
The First of January is of late esteemed
In freedom's mighty stream
When Lincoln signed the course of fate
Of which our fathers dreamed.
Memories of the day now are dim,
Of the deafening cheers and sobbing cries,
Fainting women and shouting men,
And cannons firing in the skies.
Colored and white, both exclaimed
As freedom was proclaimed
Shaking hands, marching undaunted together
Up Pennsylvania Avenue, a mile or more
On this day which means as much
Or more the July four.
Only God's Sabbath brings such joy,
As on this day which placed
Upon America's altar of civilization
The immortal claim of Emancipation.

POETS (OR WE REAL BAD)_____

poets are prophets of truth
and healing.
poets possess psychology,
that is why they are not invited to do
talk shows.
poet are dangerous.

WHO'S HELD HOSTAGE, AMERICA?

We came against our will.
Dragged from our homeland,
Led across history's waters,
Under a death ship's mast,
To these shores anchored fast.
Who is held hostage, America?

Our bodies were shackled,
But not our spirits,
And not our minds.
We resisted our capture,
And steeled our wills hard,
Prayed to God,
Cursing unknown devils.
Who is held hostage, America?

Bodies in the wind,
Swing back and forth,
Crosses in the yard,
Burnt and charred,
Fear in our hearts
Where joy should abound,
Chased by phantom hoods,
Hunted by the hounds

Despite all this,
We withstood the test,
Even more than the rest.
(For America-working,
digging, sowing, rigging)
America, a magnificent dream.
America, built on a stream of two hundred
years.

(For America, laying the tracks)
America, built on our backs.
Who is held hostage, America?

Four fifths man, owning no land,
Jim Crowed, ghetto-ised,
We listened to all the lies,
And witnessed the separate,
But equal creature feature,
(Unchaining the laws)-
Why can't we start
To unchain the hearts,
Abominations in a Christian nation.

Last hired, first fired.
Welfare rolls
Holes in our shoes, creating the blues.
You pimped our women
And shamed our men
Can't you see what shape
We're in? you're in?
Who is held hostage, America?

*SISTERS GOTTA LISTEN*_____

Sisters gotta listen
To a sister like her
Her work is never done
Still she hears the drum

Sisters gotta know
Of a sister like her
Who races with the sun
To see her teaching done

Sisters gotta feel
Like a sister like her
That mountains are high
So she can touch the sky

A THANK YOU NOTE TO MARTIN LUTHER KING, JR._____

I put on your voice
and listen
to the thunders of your truth
in your words
in your life
adding energy to my soul
 propelling me
toward compassion
toward reason
toward creative action
I remember you
you served the people.
God rest your soul—
but never shall the day
still your voice. Amen

NEW YORK CITY

New York City
is moving
whether
you
move or not
in the fire
of summer
or ice of snow days
New York
moves
The city never stops

THE LAND DOES NOT KNOW WHO OWNS IT

There are plots and lots
plantations and nations
but the land
does not know
who owns it
And the air
calls no place
home

*PASSING BEYOND VANITY*_____

I am still
concerned
with how I look
And yet all these years
have me know
I cannot see
me
truly.
For mirrors
show me differently
by light
by quality
nothing exact
they show
and some I like
Some I abhor
But all these faces
are me and more
much more
I shall be
even more
you see
when I pass
beyond vanity

GROWING OLD

Growing old is
the fulfillment
of myself
a feast
of freedom
from the fears and frills
of earlier times.

Growing old is
serenity in shades;
fastened memories
forever cherished,
and feelings tuned
more softly.
Growing old is
a gift.

FOR MY SISTERS WHO WANT TO BE FREE

The difference between
desire and being
is courage
The way to the end
of the road
is to walk with your sisters,
To call your mothers back
from slavery
Action is liberating
Strength is persistence—

Now is already yesterday
And your sons want your liberty
So they can be men.

*ROOTED*_____

Movements that began
with our walk earlier
holding hands through backyards
In the slow seduction
of our evening
As we both
Knew where we would end up.
Even if we lose the rhythm
momentarily
It is more than I can stand
Just to have this dance
In you
With you—
How come I never felt
this
before
No matter how many times before.
And it is easy
Just being with you
Before being in you
of you
with you
Rooted
Like this.

*JESUS OF THE FAVELA*_____

Jesus of the Favela
coming toward me fast;
stopped a moment
and stared at me
then he darted past.
What cruel pain was his,
what weight to carry so.
I know my God is merciful
but Sorrow, does she know?

THE GHOSTS OF WAR_____

They move on battlefield and shore
Evading eyes that do not know;
Transfixed in time, in history's grasp
Forever caught up in the past.

Some on watch where shadows lie
No sound of battle, no war cry.
Brave men all on each side pause
To fight for home, to fight for cause

The scenes enact themselves again.
War makes ghosts of lots of men.
Swamps, hills and the river bed
Play host to those yet undead.

*YOUR SMILE, YOUR STYLE*_____

For Sister Julian with Love

I'll remember your smile
I'll remember your style
I'll remember how you entered my day
Your sunshine pushed the clouds away
Could anyone forget
That you made them better
Than they were before you came.
Tomorrow will never frown
on my memories of you
And I will hear your clear gentle voice
Telling me do more be more
Oh, I will remember you
I'll remember your smile
I'll remember your style
To be sure.

*IF WE FORGET*_____

If we forget
Who will keep the dream?
Who will celebrate?

Ancient portraits in black
Reaching back
Reaching forward to today
Timbuktu, Zimbabwe

If we forget
Who will keep the dream?
Who will celebrate?

If we forget
Who will care?
Who will share our pyramids,
store our past,
See our glory?
Share our story.
Who will celebrate
Malcolm and Martin
Whitney, and Washington
Lincoln and Hampton
Tuskegee
Destinations, destiny?
Who will remember?

Who will remember?
Who will remember?
Who will remember me?
If we forget
Who will remember
Shades of black
Reaching forward, reaching back
Ebony echoes growing strong

Singing songs
In the night
Richard Wright
Slavery's sorrow
Slavery's pain
Freedom's struggle
Freedom's gain
Tubman's train
Bethune and Brooke
Gwendolyn's book
W.E.B. and Owen's too
Billie's blues and Hughes's blues
If we forget
Who will keep the dream?
Who will celebrate?
Who will remember
Roberson
Muhammed won
Burt's fun and Anderson
Marshall's Law
Pushkin and Dumas?
How far?
Can we go
If we forget
If we forget
Who will remember?
Who will celebrate?

WHEN I FELL

When I fell
and cut my knee
There was no one there
To laugh at me
And no one there
to ease the pain
And so I cried aloud,
in vain.

*BLACK GENERATION*_____

Dedicated to T. X. Jahannes

The generations
from African Eve to
African Solomon
from African Sheba
to Ras Tafari
from Shaka Zulu
to Kwame Nkrumah
from W.E.B.
to Malcolm and Martin

Countless generations
of fathers and mothers
of legend and courage

We invoke your voices.
Speak!

Stop, my Black Generation,
Doing what you're doing
If it's going to bring you ruin

Stop, my Black Generation,
Running each other down
Being our own slaves
And slave masters.

We need to activate minds
And inflame spirits

Stop, my Black Generation,
Blaming the bigots
Bigots don't kill the dream
Half as much as ignorance

212

And self-flagellation

Stop being headed for self-destruction
Don't fall into the trap described in the rap

Stop, my Black Generation,
Listening to bad press
Seeing gross absurdities
And believing it is us

Stop, my Black Generation,
The Death in our neighborhoods,
Terror on the reign,
Blacks killing blacks like they're going insane.
Mothers without mercy
Fathers without bail
Mere children sent to jail

Stop, my Black Generation,
Confusing maleness and manhood,
Fathering fatherless children

And stop
Mistaking black culture
For dressing up like pimps and streetwalkers
Or, for the pseudo cultural consciousness
Of copycat leather medallions and dashiki
(for show only)
Of Nefertiti chains without Nefertiti brains
Don't just dress up our behinds, impress our
minds.

Stop
Letting our egos and agendas
Hinder us from a master plan
Strategize!
If you don't stand together for something

You stand to lose everything

Stop
Massaging our minds with rhetoric
About revolution
Change takes practice, practice produces
revolution

Stop
Mistaking leadership for showmanship
Leadership is getting somebody else
From someplace to someplace else

If you are only managing to get yourself seen
You ain't no leader

And, understand the expressive power
of Black
language
Understand the ethno-idiosyncratic use
of Black language
It's all right to say "ain't no leader"
If you understand it means
You are not, never, were, and
Probably never will be

Stop, my Black Generation,
Ignoring the naked, the desperate,
the destitute
The commandment is clear:
"Love thy neighbor as thyself"

Stop, my Black Generation,
The drug pushers, downtown
And on the high seas,
With Wall Street connections
And government subsidies

Bringing their cargo planes of dope
To our neighborhoods
As quick fixes for ailing spirits
Stop, Black mothers,
Closing your eyes when your sons deal crack
"Cause you value the money
they bring home
More than you value the home

Stop, my Black Generation,
The giving of needles to homeless junkies
When we should be giving jobs to the jobless
And homes to the homeless;
Affordable housing for everyone

Stop, my Black Generation,
The stockpiling of food in silos,
The trading of grain for spies
When people are starving
And the belly of Ethiopia is dressed
With skin tight wire ribs and eyes of death

Stop, my Black Generation,
Cheating our children of schools and tools
Giving the British Knights, Gucci bags and
Stacey Adams
When we should be teaching them the 4 "R"s
Reading, 'Riting, 'Rithmetic and Respect

What we do with children
Is more important
than what we do for children

Children copy what they see
And repeat what they learn

Stop, my Black Generation,

215

Whispering our worries alone in the night
The sun goes down much too quick,
Daylight's eye is harsh and plain.
Let's get busy and mend the years;
Let's get strong and stop the tears;
Let's get wise and shake our fears

Stop, my Black Generation,
Quibbling over whether we are African
Americans
Or, Americans of African descent
Labels are limited, time flies
The work's yet to be done

Stop, my Black Generation,
Apologizing for the beauty of Black life
While others steal our words
And coin our ideas
Dance our dances, sing our songs
Walk our walk, talk our talk
Pick our brains, gain our gains

Stop, my Black Sisters!
Thinking the liberation of our women
Is separate from the liberation of our families
No "one" can be free when no one is free.

Know what I'm saying.

Stop, my Black Generation,
Pumping up our celebrities
While their dues are overdue
And their commitments replaced by "IOU"

Stop, my Black Generation,
The building of nuclear reactors
(Be human benefactors)

Only the sane will survive

Stop, my Black Generation,
Pretending plagues don't come to America
'Cause we got one now
(courting a man-made
Retro-virus; holding hands
with dis-integration)
'Cause sex without love is sin
And the CDC will CIA and FBI us to death

Stop, my Black Generation,
Misunderstanding ethno-economics
A dollar in the hands of our own
Ought to be a dollar in our own hands

Stop, my Black Generation,
Abandoning our small farms
Who will feed us
When we cannot feed ourselves

Stop, my Black Generation,
Letting our teachers be casualties
Of institutional expulsion,
Or Missing-In-Action
When our children need models
And mentors with minds

Stop, my Black Generation,
The rituals of religion
Congregating for social form
Serving pews, and choirs
and chicken feasting
With petty preachers
who court our pretty sisters
And steal our investment capital
When they should be healers of the mind

217

'Cause truth is in the Word
And the truth shall set you …. what?
(All God's children's got brains!)

Stop, my Black Generation,
Joining armies of containment,
Armies of contentment
We should be building (recruiting) (raising)
Armies of liberation

Stop, my Black Generation,
Singing the old funeral hymns and lullabies
"We Shall Overcome"—Someday?
Let a brave new song be sung
A song of passion, a song of power

Let it sing in our hearts
Echoing the strength of our generations.

Stop, my Black Generation,
Strangling ourselves with stress
Feeling we must be "mono"-lithic,
"Bi"-lingual, "multi'-intellectual

Stop, my Black Generation,
Celebrating our dead heroes
Count the everyday survivors as heroes
(Without popped out veins and formaldehyde
brains)
our mothers and fathers, and us

Stop, my Black Generation,
Ignoring our poets
Poets are prophets of truth and healing
Poets possess psychology

Stop, my Black Generation,

Refusing to reconnect with mother Africa
When Africa is underdeveloped
And we are
underemployed
And underrealized

Stop
Cutting ourselves off from other Africans
in the Americas
And in islands of the Caribbean
The same roots spring eternal
The same pain, the same hunger,
the same hope!

Stop, my Black Generation,
Letting others write our history
While they glorify their mythology

Stop, my Black Generation,
Sleeping through America's promise
With a check uncashed
And curses unsaid
Loans denied
And young born dead

Take control, take control
(If we know better, we can be better.)

Stop, my Black Generation,
Asking what we can do for our country
And ask what we can do for ourselves
Then our country will be better served

Stop, my Black Generation,
Possessing awesome intellects and skills,
Giving the last drop to IBM and Company
When the altar of our needs is not served

"Oh Say Can You See
By the dawn's early light"
That somebody's already up,
In the backrooms and boardrooms
Fixing the fight

Stop, my Black Generation,
And realize we may have to save America
From herself

Nothing is without us,
Everything is within us

Stop, my Black Generation,
Waiting for anybody to give us a signal
We can only be free if we free ourselves

Stop, my Black Generation,
Resisting the spirit world
Which brought us over
And binds our children's future

In the Beginning,
There was Darkness
And the Darkness stepped out
on nothingness
Coming out of nowhere
Connecting us with eternity

Knowledge is power,
Science is servant
Wisdom is free
Freedom is everything!

Iron rots
Rivers run dry

Mountains heave and mountains sigh

But, ours is the power and the promise!
The power and the promise
The power and the promise
All eyes must see one vision!
We will be free, we must be free!

*IF THEY CUT DOWN THE TREE_*
(or Limited Thoughts)

If they cut down the tree
Where will the birds go?
If the birds go away
Who will sing in the evenings?
If there is no signing
How will I live?

*LITTLE DARK-EYED GIRL*_____

For Gloria Cerestine on her birthday

Little dark-eyed girl
with dimpled cheeks
and a soft smile,
do I love you, you ask?
Do I love you?
What a silly question.

I know I never seem to have time
to touch and caress you.
I know.
I ask about your day and play,
but never listen to what you say.
I buy you things that make the pretty you
so pretty
but seem not to see you.
No swinging around or tickling—
No time, no time, no time
for love, you say.

Little dark-eyed girl
with dimpled cheeks
and a soft smile,
do I love you, you ask?
Do I love you?
What a silly question.
Trust my heart—

KEEP THE DREAM

Keep the dream
And our children will be free
Keep the dream
And our children will know joy
Keep the dream
And our children will be safe
Keep the dream
And our children will be loved
Keep the dream
And our children will keep the dream

*LOOK BACK IN SHAME*_____

When the new century's come
And justice is finally true
The brothers of the lighter hue
Will celebrate the strength of you
And look back in shame
Over the rough road we came
They shall ultimately see
The sheer devilish lunacy
Of their forefathers of today
Who tried to steal our rights away
They shall look back in shame
Have no doubt, no doubt
For goodness shall will out
And strength has kept us this day
Strength shall keep up all the way.

DREAM MAKER

I know the dream
I am a foolproof plan to own tomorrow.
I have patience and persistent vision
and daring
all in the same season.
I am not the keeper of the dream,
though I cherish it.
I am the dream maker

*AIN'T I SOMETHING*_____

My blood is thick
My mind is quick
Ain't I Somethin'
Ain't I Somethin'
My head is clear
My back is strong
My song is long
Ain't I Somethin'
Ain't I Somethin'
Something so real
That I can feel it
Ain't I Somethin'
The world is mine
My dreams are old
My life is bold
Ain't I Somethin'
Ain't I Somethin'

I will be strong
I will be free
Love and joy,
A part of me
Ain't I Somethin'
Ain't I Somethin'
Ain't I Somethin'
Ain't I Somethin'

KING CAT AND ALL THAT_____

Once there was a huge and haughty lion
Whose weight made the jungle sway.
A little mouse, it is told,
one day came into the lion's way.
The lion caught the mouse
in his large, heavy paw,
and he laughed as the mouse
squirmed and squealed,
"Hah, hah,! Hah, hah!"

The mouse said "Please let me go,
kind sir!
You are hurting me,"
The lion squeezed him more
and stomped upon the jungle floor.

"Please set me free,
don't hurt me",
cried the mouse,
sorry now he'd ever
left his house, this day.

"I am the king of the jungle,
the master of beasts",
said the lion.
"I'll do what I please.
I am strong and powerful.
I am mighty and all that",
boasted the king cat.

The mouse tried to move
to no avail,
caught tight was he.

But, as the lion continued his play,

he loosened his grip
and the mouse
in a swish
got away.

Later that day
near sun set
the lion was caught
like that
in a net
and catapulted up a tree.

Needless to say
King lion growled and roared,
growled and roared
and tried to get free
to no avail,
caught tight was he
up a tree.

As it happened,
our friend the mouse
ventured again
from his house.

Hearing a howling, growling
and a roaring on the trail,
the mouse
cautiously
made his way there to see.

And what did he see?
King Cat up a tree.

"Oh! It is not you Mister Lion?
strong, Mister Lion!
Oh, it's not you Mister Cat,

powerful and mighty and all that.
It's not you, King of Beast,
that I see
up a tree? said the mouse.

After a little laugh
the mouse scampered
up the tree
and gnawed the rope
until the lion fell free.

The lion crashed
to the ground
on his big behind.

The little mouse looked
down at the lion and said,
"Oh how can it be
that little me
set you free?"
The lion bowed his head.
Nothing more was said.

GOD

I done converted God
from a father to a friend
so he can see
what trouble we is in

MY CHILDREN
HAVE NEVER KNOWN PEACE___

My children have never known peace
My children have never been to sleep
without fear
My children have no visions
of kingdoms of joy
My children have been steeped too early
in the harsh brine of truth
My children have been steeled too early
in forced hard emotions
My children cough
too many bitter soliloquies
My children are given no time for dreams
If I could give them one gift
It would be a news report that peace had
broken out and claimed them
It would be an answer to their anger
It would be an equation to end the self-doubt
that disturbs their youth
It would be pages in a treasure book
in which to write their hopes
It would be a village
surrounded by even chances
It would be the luxury to play games
without penalties
It saddens my soul that my children
are captives
quartered between justice denied
and wanton greed
where they stand weaponless
I would make them a pledge
Not to sleep until peace comes
Not to sit down until peace comes

Not to smile until peace comes
Not to bargain with anybody
who stands in
the way of their peace
Not to give refuge to my own brother
and sister if they are enemies of the peace
Not to regret any action
I must take to give them peace
Not to let any man rest
who steals their peace
My children have never known peace
and I will die trying to help them find it in
their own backyards
 so I can see them hug each other as they yearn to do
so I can hear sweet poetry fall
from their tongues
so I can see them feast
in the glorious freshness of their age
so I can hear them season
the lyrics of their songs
so I can see nourish their unrealized genius
so I can see them fall down with laughter

ON THE JOY OF READING TO YOUNG BLACK CHILDREN_____

Hoping to inspire some Langston Hughes
or Sonia Sanchez or Tony Medina
in what appears
to be rubble producing neighborhoods
I read to youngsters at the local library
If one of them could be touched by one word
maybe the word would become life
sending a gift-child on his way
paying my token for entry into heaven.
I read
to eyes that give me back the pages
reading stories in and out of them
hoping to awaken in young souls
dreams that will dwell in tomorrow's light
Help me, God, to read better than anything
I do not want to miss Richard Wright
or James Brown
or Smokey Robinson, or Nona Hendryx
make me read with a joy
to unlock the universe

TOGETHER

For Andrea

And
Now that we
have come to the end
of this time and place
my friend
how shall we spend
the future?

We cannot ever be
sure
of the times ahead
but let it always
be said
We were very together
then
When
it mattered.

AUTHOR

Ja A. Jahannes is a poet, playwright, essayist, novelist, librettist, composer, spoken word artist, social critic, psychologist, and educator. He received a B. A. degree with honors from Lincoln University (PA), two Master's degrees from Hampton University and a Ph.D. from the University of Delaware. He is a frequent writer, columnist, and contributing editor for numerous national and international publications. Jahannes has received many awards. He has written and produced twelve plays and published two books, a collection of essays, over two hundred articles, reviews, and poems, two oratorios, two symphony librettos, two opera librettos, a song cycle, and the recent memoir anthology *WordSong Poets*. He is the author of three novels, **Big Man**, **The Prayer Stone**, and **Sabbath Run**. Jahannes has also written lyrics for over 100 songs and directed many theatre and performance productions, touring in the U. S. and abroad. He is a BMI publisher and writer. He is listed in the "Top Forty Contemporary Poets In The World." Jahannes has lectured in Africa, Asia, South America, the Caribbean, the Middle East and Europe.

www.ingramcontent.com/pod-product-compliance
Lightning Source LLC
LaVergne TN
LVHW011152080426
835508LV00007B/351